What Readers Really Do

P9-DNW-597

DOROTHY BARNHOUSE & VICKI VINTON

What Readers Really Do

Teaching the Process of Meaning Making

HEINEMANN
Portsmouth, NH

Heinemann
361 Hanover Street
Portsmouth, NH 03801–3912
www.heinemann.com

Offices and agents throughout the world

© 2012 by Dorothy Barnhouse and Vicki Vinton

All rights reserved. No part of this book may be reproduced in any form or by any electronic or mechanical means, including information storage and retrieval systems, without permission in writing from the publisher, except by a reviewer, who may quote brief passages in a review, and with the exception of reproducible pages (identified by the *What Readers Really Do* copyright line), which may be photocopied for classroom use only.

"Dedicated to Teachers" is a trademark of Greenwood Publishing Group, Inc.

The authors and publisher wish to thank those who have generously given permission to reprint borrowed material:

"The First Day of Spring" from *Fresh Paint: New Poems* by Eve Merriam. Copyright © 1986 by Eve Merriam. Reprinted by permission of Marian Reiner.

"Food. Music. Memory." by Susan Marie Scavo. Copyright © 1999 by Susan Marie Scavo. Reprinted by permission of the author.

Excerpts from *Pictures of Hollis Woods* by Patricia Reilly Giff. Copyright © 2002 by Patricia Reilly Giff. Used by permission of Wendy Lamb Books, an imprint of Random House Children's Books, a division of Random House, Inc.

Library of Congress Cataloging-in-Publication Data
Barnhouse, Dorothy (Dorothy J.)
   What readers really do : teaching the process of meaning making / Dorothy Barnhouse and Vicki Vinton.
      p. cm.
   Includes bibliographical references.
   ISBN-13: 978-0-325-03073-9
   ISBN-10: 0-325-03073-1
   1. Reading (Elementary). 2. Reading (Middle school). 3. Reading comprehension.
4. Thought and thinking. I. Vinton, Vicki. II. Title.
LB1573.B3584 2012
372.4—dc23   2011039445

Editor: Margaret LaRaia
Production: Lynne Costa
Cover and text designs: Monica Ann Crigler
Front cover photograph: Dynamic Graphics/Jupiter Images/Getty/HIP
Back cover photograph: Stockbyte/Getty Images/HIP
Typesetter: Valerie Levy, Drawing Board Studios
Manufacturing: Steve Bernier

Printed in the United States of America on acid-free paper
16   15   14   13   VP   3   4   5

For my father who read to me,

and my mother who took me to the library.

DB

To David—

for all the reasons you know and more.

VV

Contents

CHAPTER TWO: What We Mean by Meaning Making: Noticing and Naming What We Do as Readers **32**

We invite you into a workshop we've conducted with teachers that examines how readers make meaning in a text. We look at three strands of thinking involved in this process— comprehension, understanding, and evaluation—and notice how much of our reading is a process of drafting and revising to reach these different layers of meaning. We then consider what we know about how texts work that helps us do this, and how we can apply that knowledge to the texts our students are reading.

SECTION 2: STEPPING INTO CLASSROOMS

CHAPTER THREE: How Readers Draft and Revise Their Way from Confusion to Clarity **51**

We introduce a fifth-grade student who causes us to look closely at the thinking readers do when first starting a book: how confusion is a natural by-product of reading narratives and how readers draft and revise their thinking as a result. We then go into a third-grade classroom where we demonstrate a lesson that teaches students to do this with greater awareness, and unpack some of our teaching moves. We conclude with a follow-up small-group lesson that steps students up to comprehend textual clues in more complex texts.

CHAPTER FOUR: How Readers Infer the Significance of Details   76

A small group of fifth graders we're working with makes us reflect on the role details play in texts and how readers know which ones are significant. We then teach a seventh-grade class how to infer significance by connecting details, and examine the methodology we use to do this. We end by demonstrating a small-group lesson that grounds students in the details of a text in order to consider bigger ideas at play.

CHAPTER FIVE: How Readers Look Closely at Patterns to Draft Understandings   106

We talk with a fourth-grade teacher about a group of students in a book club who seem to be missing the deeper layers in their book and ponder how readers move beyond comprehension to understanding. We then teach a fifth-grade class to "see" what a text might be "telling" them by noticing, tracking, and connecting patterns, and highlight the teaching moves that allow students to construct rather than identify meaning. We conclude by looking more closely at the role of patterns in texts during a one-on-one conference with a student.

CHAPTER SIX: How Readers Put All the Parts Together to Revise Their Understandings 143

In a meeting with a fourth-grade teacher we become aware of the complexity of thinking involved in finishing a book. As a result we look more closely at the process of revision in reading. We confront this in a fourth-grade classroom with two students who move to a deeper understanding of a book's themes by reexamining patterns they've noticed. Our teaching emphasizes how flexible readers need to be during this thinking and how our methodology differs significantly from traditional teaching around theme. We then look at how to ensure that students are transferring their learning from one text to another.

CHAPTER SEVEN: How Readers Evaluate the Worth of a Text by Questioning and Considering Its Relevance 175

An end-of-book discussion with third graders forces us to look closely at how we take texts into our lives as we finish them. We return to each of the classrooms we have introduced in the previous chapters to glimpse ways we facilitate student talk that moves beyond the usual text-to-self connections and pat talk around author's message and author's purpose. We discuss how this step is the essential final step in meaning making without which students will not experience agency or transfer and talk one-on-one with a student about how to use her response to one book to help begin drafting her identity as a reader.

CODA: Learning from the Texts That Are Our Classrooms 194
We share some final reflections on what it means to be a reader and a teacher.

Acknowledgments

The path to a book is never easy and rarely simple, though to a large extent this one feels inevitable, the by-product of over two decades of working together. For these and other reasons, we chose to write this book as "we." But thankfulness comes from deep inside one's self, and we feel we can no more say "*We* thank so and so" than we can breathe or eat for each other. That said, there are a few people with whom we've worked together and we would first like to thank them, and then move into our own individual acknowledgments.

Teaching is the ultimate act of collaboration, and much of this book speaks to the power of structuring our classrooms as collaborative entities. Lucy Calkins, the Director of the Teachers College Reading and Writing Project, gave us our first glimpse of this more than twenty-five years ago. She invited us to join her at a table filled with incredible educators all committed to finding more meaningful ways to teach reading and writing and in so doing showed us the value of putting raw thoughts on the table and seeing what they could become.

Shelley Harwayne, first as co-director of the Project and then as superintendent of District 2 in Manhattan, shared with us her immense experience as a teacher and her abiding respect for children. From Shelley we learned that teaching wasn't talking to students but learning from them.

We also both had the good fortune and privilege of working together with Charlotte Butler, the instructional coordinator of the Aurora Public Schools in Aurora, Colorado, and her invincible team of district coaches and teacher leaders who were working to implement reading and writing workshop districtwide with as much integrity, thoughtfulness, and diligence as any district we've seen.

And finally, we'd like to jointly pay homage to our editor, Margaret LaRaia, who never once flagged in her belief and enthusiasm for this project. She answered distress calls and emails with more patience and grace than either of us thought possible, and showed the wisdom of Solomon as she helped us merge our visions into one. That she is a reader and an educator herself was an enormous boon as she helped us first articulate for ourselves and then for our readers the complex and mysterious process of reading. This book would not have been possible without her.

And now, there are many individual thanks we owe, for when all is said and done, "we" are two people who each leaned on many others as we made our way through the process of writing this book.

DOROTHY:

The ideas in this book would not even be words let alone lessons without the teachers and administrators who trusted in the process of collaborative study and opened their doors to me. Jackie Allen Joseph cleared a wide path for me to think out loud with the teachers she led, first as a literacy coach at PS 230 in Brooklyn and then as an assistant principal at PS 261, also in Brooklyn. Jackie's unwavering faith in the power of teachers thinking together continues to renew my faith in teaching and in public education.

Sharon Fiden and Freya Grice at PS 230 are administrators who believe it's their job to make sure that everyone who enters their school is and remains a learner, so it doesn't surprise me that they were the ones who first handed me Peter Johnston's *Choice Words*, a small book that changed my teaching, and invited me to join in on the conversations it sparked with their staff. Thanks to all the teachers there who nurtured this book during its infancy and whose words are the backbone of the *Food.Music.Memory* workshop.

The teachers at PS 261, led by Zipporiah Mills, helped the lessons in this book become a reality. The amazing CTT partners Colleen Greto and Megan Kane were thoughtful risk takers and I'm jealous of their students every day. Nicole Blyden and Jook Leung also generously opened their rooms to me, jumping head first into work that was certainly not familiar and not always comfortable. And Karen Kaz was always there, a listening partner who knew when to speak up. The conversations around the table with all the teachers in grades 3–5 were invaluable in helping me articulate and pin down my thinking. Thanks to each of you.

Many of the lessons in this book also took shape at PS 368, the Hamilton Heights School in Manhattan, with Alva Buxenbaum as the principal. I couldn't ask for better partners in collaborative inquiry than this small group of fiercely dedicated teacher-readers: Sharlene Aquiler, Amy Corsun, Sarah Johnson, Jennifer Kaiser, and Marissa Torres. At the Secondary School of Law in Brooklyn, Lisa Silva, Kim Sobel, and Lizzie Torres enabled me to see how vital this work is to the work of life, and at MS 51 in Brooklyn, Lisa Schwartz and Ryan Michele Healey plunked me down with the student reading *Identical* and listened in not just as teachers but also as readers.

My final thanks go to my husband, Jack Bales, and our daughters, Lucy and Ella. You all are really great at helping me step back from the fray and laugh—at myself, usually—which is just what I need, and you know just when.

VICKI:

Like Dorothy, I am forever indebted to the New York City public school administrators and teachers who opened up both their classrooms and their minds as, together, we tried to wrap our heads around how to help students read. In particular, I would like to acknowledge IS 111 and Baruch College Campus High School (BCCHS) as the schools where I first began experimenting with the thinking that informs this book, and offer a fond thanks and salute to former and current 111 teachers John Fanning, Deborah Berg, and Roberto Padilla, and to teachers Diane DiRico, Rita Ross, Leah Witman, and principal extraordinaire Alicia Perez at BCCHS.

The journey continued at PS 77, a.k.a. the Lower Lab School, where my thanks go to former principal Renay Sadis, whose mission it was to bring not just rigor but joy to her school's reading workshop, and to then fourth-grade teachers Maria Koutras and Barrie Schwarz who, recognizing the dangers in using a text you have taught and know inside out, challenged me to find a book for a read-aloud that neither they nor their students had read in order to better attend to and see what they actually do as readers to make meaning the first time around. My thanks also go to Lower Lab third-grade teachers Justin Connors and Donna Seferian, who joined me in modeling the discussion about Aesop that so inspired their students.

More recently, my work has taken me to PS 196 in the Bronx and PS 26 in Staten Island, two very different schools filled with smart, dedicated, risk-taking teachers. Special thanks goes to the PS 196 literacy coaches, Rosa Rahbani and Susan Horowitz, who never failed to inspire me each time we sat down to talk, and to Alison Valenci, Randy Rosen, Laura Dwyer, and Muriel Timari at PS 26, who fearlessly jumped into what Alison's students called "the big thinking" work of reading with gusto.

Finally, I'd like to express my gratitude to a handful of individuals for specific contributions to both my thinking and my life: Thank you, Michelle Ottie, from the Aurora Public Schools, for sharing with me your own thinking about assessing the demands of the text, and thank you, Ellen Kruschwitz, also from Aurora, for first noticing and naming for me that I rooted every conference I had with your students—whether it was about identifying an antecedent or re-membering a character's name—within the context of meaning-making and the deeper work of a reader. Thank you, Mimi Aronson, co-founder with Artie Voigt of Literacy Support Systems, which has arranged for much of my New York City work, for always reminding me that less is more and to trust my instincts. Thank you, Mary Ehrenworth, for simply being there as both a great friend and great colleague. Thank you, daughter Michela, for all those times you said "Don't worry, Mama," when work on this book kept me at my desk longer than I'd expected. And finally, thank you, David, for your staggering patience and your willingness to listen to me thrash out ideas or read a tricky passage, for the homemade ramen that gave me sustenance and, above all, for your love.

Introduction

Making Our Foundations and Purposes Visible

Read in order to live.

—Gustave Flaubert

Since you've opened this book, the chances are good that you're a lover of children, a lover of books, or a lover of both. You're also likely to be a learner, someone who's committed to keep growing as a thinker, believing that learning is as essential and indispensable to living as breathing. What we're sure about, though, from the simple fact that you're here alongside us on the page, is that you read. Put another way, we know you are a reader, whether what you read consists of professional books, young adult novels or children's books, newspapers, magazines, bestsellers, or blogs—anything from the back of cereal boxes to that creature called "literature."

While that may seem obvious, we think it is critical to point out here for several reasons. First and foremost, as we'll demonstrate throughout the course of the book, we believe that being a reader allows you to be an effective teacher of reading, regardless of whatever specialized training you may or may not have had. Katie Wood Ray's marvelous book about teaching writing, *What You Know by Heart* (2002), is predicated on a similar belief: that we can build meaningful curriculum and lessons based on what we know and do, in her case as writers, and in ours as readers. What's needed is a willingness to peer into the recesses of our own reader's mind, attending to the work we do internally that frequently goes unnoticed or that happens so quickly it often feels automatic—what we call the invisible work of reading—and mining our brains for those nuggets of knowledge we have about how texts work. We'll attempt to make that invisible work visible by noticing and naming what we do as readers and what we know as readers about how texts work. Additionally we'll make visible the kind of instruction we think best helps students "see" that invisible work and that also significantly allows us, as teachers, to "see" our students' minds at work, visibly thinking and making meaning as they read.

Effective Teaching: Stepping Into and Out of Our Own Heads

The other reason we believe it's important to acknowledge the fact that all of us are readers has to do with the ongoing quest to identify the factors that contribute to student achievement. What will come as no surprise to those of us who spend our days in schools is that researchers have now discovered that, more than smaller class size, more than better funding, more than higher standards or benchmarks, what affects student performance the most is the classroom teacher. This finding, in turn, has sparked a new quest to identify the specific factors that make teachers most effective. While this research is still ongoing, two components have emerged that we believe are specifically connected to the work you'll find in these pages. Robert Pianta and his team of researchers at the University of Virginia (2004), for example, point to the social and instructional interactions teachers have with students, breaking those down into three domains: emotional support, classroom organization, and instructional supports. These all, in effect, have to do with *how* we teach: how we talk to students to convey information, provide vital feedback, acknowledge their perspectives—how we nudge and coax and encourage and commend in order to create a positive learning environment based on students' strengths, not just their deficits.

The second factor has to do with *what* we teach, that is, the content of our lessons and our own store of content knowledge. There, what researchers such as Heather Hill of Harvard and Judith Lanier and Deborah Loewenberg Ball of Michigan State's School of Education have discovered is that effective teachers possess a particular kind of understanding about content that goes beyond traditional notions of what constitutes both content and pedagogical knowledge. Writing for *The New York Times Sunday Magazine* in an article titled "Building a Better Teacher" (2010), education reporter Elizabeth Green describes this in the context of Ball's work with mathematics:

> Mathematicians need to understand a problem only for themselves; math teachers need to both know the math and to know how 30 different minds might understand (or misunderstand) it. Then they need to take each mind from not getting it to mastery. And they need to do this in 45 minutes or less.

This, Green writes, requires an understanding about the subject matter that "was neither pure content knowledge nor what educators call pedagogical knowledge. . . . It was a different animal altogether," that at some point was contingent on the "ability to step outside of your own head."

As literacy teachers, we may recognize the truth in this, especially the challenge of taking sometimes more than thirty minds that all see and learn things differently from zero to sixty in a short chunk of time. But the challenge for us is compounded in several ways. In literacy, for instance, there isn't always a direct or clear-cut equivalent to the answer of a problem in math—especially when we move past basic literal comprehension to the more subjective aspects of reading, such as interpretation. This makes it trickier to know how a mind, let alone thirty different minds, might understand or misunderstand. And there's often no true consensus—at the school level let alone at the national level—about what constitutes the content of an English Language Arts classroom. Is it the books we read with our students, either as a read-aloud or a whole-class text—*Bridge to Terabithia* in fourth grade, say, or *To Kill a Mockingbird* in eighth? Is it the skills we know students need—inferring, summarizing, synthesizing, and the like? Or is it the bullet points found in standards—a knowledge of various genres and text features, literary elements and devices?

This is where being a reader is so critical. As readers we know the importance of each of these foci. We bring an understanding of how texts and genres work with us when we read, along with a repertoire of strategies and skills—though as proficient readers we frequently use them so quickly and naturally that we're barely aware of them. And, of course, there must be a text, whether it's one comprised of words or, in the case of picture books and graphic novels, images. Yet as readers we also know that, while these things are important, we don't actually read to practice inferring, identify a conflict, or learn what someone else has said—be it a teacher, a critic, or Spark Notes—about, say, the symbolism in *To Kill a Mockingbird*'s title. At best, these skills and this kind of knowledge all are means to an end, but not the end itself. We know this instinctively as readers. Yet as teachers we often present these things as the end goal of reading, while the end—the true and deeper end, the reason why we try to infer and consider things like conflict and symbols—is often not defined or made clear. It remains, again, invisible. And as such it impacts our effectiveness, depriving us of that particular kind of content knowledge we need to help our students achieve— knowledge that's within our grasp and attainable by looking more closely at ourselves as readers. Put another way, before we take that critical and needed step outside of our heads, we must step deeply into them first to see more clearly what it is that we know and do as readers in order to better help our students. Only then, we believe, will we be able to help children build the enduring and strong content knowledge that the Common Core State Standards cite as one of the capacities of students who are college and career ready.

Our Paths to Becoming Teachers of Reading

This book is the culmination of a journey that began over twenty years ago when we both were graduate students at Columbia University, working toward a master of fine arts degree in writing. One day as we stood in the departmental office, perusing the bulletin board, we spied a notice that had been posted by the Teachers College Writing Project, which was looking for writers to join them in their work in the New York City public schools. Little did we know then that responding to that notice would set us on our life's work—work that has often been challenging, but has always been deeply rewarding.

At the Project, we met other writers, such as Georgia Heard and Ralph Fletcher, who had heeded the same call as we had. And we met a team of amazing educators, such as Shelley Harwayne, Lucy Calkins, Martha Horn, Joanne Hindley, and Isoke Nia, whose passion for helping children see and feel the power and joys of writing made us want to join their ranks. From them and others like them we began to learn the *how* of teaching: how to turn a classroom into a workshop where students were actively practicing and engaging in the work that real writers do; how to listen and talk to children while conferring in ways that helped them both to see and stretch themselves as writers; how to design and offer instruction that promoted and supported independence.

As for the *what*, we drew from our own understanding and practice of writing, helping the Project develop their ideas around things such as genre studies, craft lessons, and the use of writer's notebooks. When it came to reading, however, we initially took many of our content cues from others. In the early years, this included such seminal thinkers as Ken and Yetta Goodman and Ralph Peterson and Maryann Eeds, whose classic book *Grand Conversations: Literature Groups in Action* (2007) inspires us to this day. Later we turned to educators such as Ellin Keene, Stephanie Harvey, and the esteemed Brian Cambourne, all of whom introduced us to the body of research upon which both strategy instruction and the balanced literacy approach stand.

We're indebted to all these thinkers and writers who've informed and helped shape our thinking, but the more time we spent in classrooms, as staff developers, consultants, and coaches working in New York City schools and districts around the country, the more we found ourselves turning to our own experience as readers, which went back a lifetime. As children we both were readers of the flashlight-under-the-covers-long-after-bedtime variety, while as adults, we recognized ourselves as the kind of reader that Anne Lamott describes in her wonderful book about writing, *Bird by Bird* (1995):

> For some of us, books are as important as almost anything else on earth. What a miracle it is that out of these small, flat, rigid squares of paper unfolds world after world after world, worlds that sing to you, comfort and quiet or excite you. Books help us understand who we are and how we are to behave. They show us what community and friendship mean; they show us how to live and die. . . . My gratitude for good writing is unbounded; I'm grateful for it the way I'm grateful for the ocean. Aren't you? (p. 15)

To be honest, we're not sure why we didn't draw on our own experience earlier. We certainly shared with teachers and children what we knew about reading like a writer, demonstrating how writers read for craft and the beauty and power of language. But rarely did we talk about reading like a reader. Perhaps it was precisely because there was so much research and theory surrounding reading, so many treatises, so many studies, all chock-full of data. Or perhaps it was because there was no trailblazer forging the way through that thicket of theory as Donald Murray did over twenty-five years ago when *A Writer Teaches Writing* (1985) first appeared and empowered those of us who wrote to ground our teaching in what we knew, not in what someone else said. Or perhaps it was simply a matter of trust or a lack thereof, a fear that we couldn't possibly be experts if, in our own reading, we sometimes failed to see what some other reader saw or didn't quite "get" whatever a critic—or the teacher's guide—said was the point. We knew, however, that, as Vicki Spandel writes in her glorious preface to *The 9 Rights of Every Writer* (2005), "fear is a poor place from which to . . . teach. It kills the very things we need most to [be] successful: genuine curiosity, tolerance of early efforts, trust in our own vision, willingness to take risk, focus on personal questions, and passion . . ." (p. xii). And so we shrugged off all those doubts and reservations, those voices in our heads that questioned our authority, and began to teach from our own lives as readers, trusting our own vision and experience.

Having taken that step, we use our experience in a variety of ways. We use it, for instance, as a barometer to gauge the authenticity of what we ask children to do, by always asking ourselves the question: Do we as readers do this, and if so, why and how? We use it, as well, to better understand virtually everything readers need to do, from figuring out what a pronoun refers to in order to comprehend a sentence to constructing a thematic understanding of a book-length text. And we use it to establish that enduring understanding, that all-important end, which all those skills and strategies and terms need to be visibly attached to: that books help us understand ourselves and the world around us, giving us glimmers of who we are and who we might become.

What we don't do, however, is use our experience to direct or guide students toward our own understanding of any given text. This is critical for several reasons—especially if you're a teacher, as we are, who aims for and values student independence. First, our understanding of any text we teach has usually been constructed, developed, and honed over time through multiple readings and exposures. We know, in part, what details are significant and what scenes are pivotal because we know how the text ends and have seen how the pieces all fit together, in a way no reader encountering a text for the first time could possibly see. Second, what we bring to a text is inevitably different than what our students bring. We are older, for one thing, with more experience up our sleeves. Some of us have partners, some of us have children, all of us have jobs, and all of us have made the transition from childhood to adulthood, with all of the pain and responsibilities and hard-won insight that entails. It is unrealistic to think that our students would see the same things we are able to see for that reason alone.

Most essentially, we refrain from dangling our own understanding of a text in front of students because of how we envision our role and stance as teachers in a classroom. As Randy Bomer so eloquently wrote in his book *Time for Meaning* (1995), we've committed ourselves to shifting our role from "the teacherly self-concept of curator or gatekeeper of content"—i.e., the one with the "right" answers, or the authority on the text—to someone "concerned primarily with students' ability to make meaning from their lives" (p. 9). Put another way, we don't want students to take on or consume our own interpretations of texts; we want them to construct their own. This means that we need to teach each student the *way* readers think as they read, not *what* to think, helping them to experience texts as readers, rather than putting specific thoughts about a text in their heads.

As we have attempted to shift our practice to reflect this vision, we have had to reexamine how we teach. For if we are not the "curators of content" in our classrooms, what is our role? And if we are not the ones with the "right" answers, how does our methodology and language have to change? In attempting to answer these questions, we have been influenced by Peter Johnston's gem of a book, *Choice Words* (2004), which explores the impact of language on student learning. The framework he describes, of noticing and naming what students do in order to build agency, identity, and flexibility, has challenged us to more directly correlate the "what" and the "how" of our teaching, and inspired us to more deeply connect the reader and the teacher within ourselves.

How to Use This Book

BECOMING A PARTICIPANT

Our journey toward this book has also been helped by the teachers we have had the good fortune of working with. Teaching is often such an isolating business; you are more often than not alone in a classroom with your students. Grappling with and sharing information and insights from colleagues is often relegated to sparsely scheduled meetings or done in a catch-as-catch-can manner, passing each other in the hall, over a rushed lunch, or in the moments before your students pour in to your room and command your attention. Rarely are teachers given opportunities to visit each other's classrooms in a spirit of study.

We've been able to work in a different way, always side by side with teachers in their classrooms, and usually for the purposes of study. This has enabled us to step back and observe—observe instruction and observe students as they work— which has been essential for our learning and growth. In writing this book we hope to afford you some of these same privileges—of working next to teachers and alongside students. To do this we have structured the chapters as a kind of study group that we'd like to invite you to join.

We start, in Chapter 1, by considering what it means to "get" a text. We do this by listening in on some conversations with student readers who show us how current practices in reading instruction do and don't allow for this to happen. In Chapter 2 we look closely at what it means to read, trying to make this most invisible of thinking processes visible for ourselves. We do this by re-creating a workshop where we attempt to "see" what readers know and do to create significant, personally relevant meaning from a text. Along the way we attempt to untangle a few terms—words like *comprehension*, *interpretation*, and *understanding*—that are often used interchangeably in classrooms and in standards that guide instruction. In Chapters 3 through 7 we take you inside some of the classrooms we have worked in. Here, we use what we have noticed and named in Chapter 2 as the lens through which we look at reading instruction. These chapters are organized in the following way:

Introductory Observation. We start these chapters by observing a student or a situation that has caused us to question or reconsider something.

What We Do as Readers. We then think about the implications of those observations by anchoring our thinking in what we know and do in our own reading.

What This Sounds Like in Classrooms. In these sections we re-create lessons we taught that attempt to address the issues we have observed. You'll notice some callout boxes in the margins of these sections. These emphasize specific teaching moves and decisions we have made that we unpack in the *What We Do as Teachers* section that follows.

What We Do as Teachers. These are the sections where we unpack our teaching, thinking aloud in an attempt to make more explicit the purposes behind the decisions we made about what and how we teach. We also look at how what we do differs from some common practices found in many classrooms—some of which we used to do ourselves. We highlight these points in margin boxes we have labeled *Rethinking Our Practice*, and additionally provide a sidebar in these chapters that names these shifts in thinking so as to make them more visible and transferable to your own students, classrooms, and texts.

Making Every Student's Thinking Visible. We conclude each of these chapters with additional instructional ideas and examples that can scaffold and/or challenge those students who reflect the full range of learners found in diverse classrooms.

We conclude with a coda that takes stock of and reflects on the importance of agency for our students and for ourselves as their teachers, and we provide templates for some of the tools we use in the Appendices, which are also available online at: heinemann.com/products/E03073.aspx.

USING EXAMPLES FROM MULTIPLE CLASSROOMS AND MULTIPLE TEXTS

You will notice that the sample lessons in Chapters 3 through 7 are from different classrooms, with different grades and cohorts of students working in different texts. We do this in order to make clearer how the process of meaning making can apply to every grade and many different texts. In each example, you'll see us offering instruction that focuses explicitly on the way a reader comes to understand a text and what they draw on to do that. We share in these pages some of the everyday language we use with students and the structures, supports, and tools we've designed to scaffold student thinking as we attempt to make big concepts accessible. We do so, however, without expecting or wanting you to follow these examples as scripts. Rather, we hope that by hearing our words you will be able to "see" our thinking and how we are attempting to articulate and communicate knowledge about texts and the reading process in a way that builds students' confidence, engagement, and growth as well as yours.

Three Philosophical Underpinnings of This Book

THE RATIONALE BEHIND NARRATIVE TEXTS

Before we delve into the meat of the book, we think it's important to provide a few caveats and explanations about the content of what you'll find. It is important to note, first, that in the classroom examples, we focus almost exclusively on book-length narrative texts, with the occasional use of excerpts. While we are confident that the broad thinking work portrayed in this book can be applied to any text—whether a poem, a short story, a film, or an expository text—we have chosen narratives as our examples for several reasons.

First, we believe that narratives, and specifically book-length narratives, help student readers practice stamina and learn to sustain comprehension. There are, for example, details to keep track of across many pages; there is development of those details; there are often multiple characters and plot lines to keep track of and make sense of; there are complicated narrative techniques, such as movement through time and differing points of view; and of course book-length narratives often explore multiple themes—a word we'll explore starting in Chapter 2—that allow different access ramps from which to construct meaning. All of these present challenges and opportunities to readers who, as the Common Core State Standards demand, need to be reading increasingly complex texts.

Narrative is also the genre that most teachers spend most of their time teaching and that most students spend most of their time reading. As we write this, there is a wide discussion in schools and among educational leaders about whether this is a good thing, and that perhaps students might be better served—in preparation for standardized tests, for content area subjects, for jobs and careers—if they were taught to read less narrative and more expository texts. While we believe that students need experience in a wide variety of texts, for many reasons we believe that teaching students to read narrative texts is not only a good thing but an essential thing. As we'll explore in depth in this book, narrative texts convey information and purpose in far more indirect and subtle ways—through language, gestures, and images—than many expository texts do. They also convey layers of meaning, with plots and characters coming together in ways that signify ideas and themes. Narrative texts operate, in these ways, as a kind of metaphor—a concept we will delve into in Chapter 6—with the story standing for something larger than its particulars, which both invites and demands that readers "read between the lines" to comprehend, interpret, appraise, and assess. Teaching narrative, then, is teaching high-level thinking.

Teaching narrative is also teaching empathy. Stories allow readers to throw their hearts and minds into the lives of others, to live, temporarily, as others live—and to learn from that. This is no small matter in educating students who will be citizens, leaders, and caretakers of our world. In fact, Columbia University School of Medicine decided this was no small matter in educating students who were going to become doctors. In 2009, they launched a new degree program, the first of its kind, called "Narrative Medicine," in part in response to the highly technical aspects of the modern medical system that, according to their website, "has all but forgotten the critical importance of stories: stories of suffering, stories of healing, stories of the relationships that tie patients to their clinicians."

THE BALANCED LITERACY APPROACH

Most of the work we've done in classrooms—whether it be in suburban New Jersey, the Rocky Mountains, or our hometown of Brooklyn—is set within the context of the balanced literacy approach, which combines read-alouds with shared reading, small-group work, and independent reading in order to support and release responsibility for learning to the students over time, with independence as the overarching goal. We don't, however, provide a primer on balanced literacy in this book; instead we share here a brief description of how we use the three components found most often in our work, and invite you to consult one or more of the professional texts we list in our bibliography should you wish to learn more.

With read-alouds, the teacher reads a text out loud to the whole class that not every student is able to navigate and read fluently on their own. This allows everyone in the room to engage in the work—and enjoyment—of making meaning without struggling to decode. Traditionally, read-aloud has been used to build community and engagement through the reading of a compelling text, but we expand on that to use it, as well, to introduce students to the big vision and process of reading we'll map out in depth in Chapter 2. We use the small-group structure for a variety of reasons, all of which center around offering students, whatever their needs, more time, support, and challenges than the whole-class read-aloud instruction allows. We bring students who we suspect might not be able to negotiate the comprehension demands of the read-aloud text on their own together for additional practice, using texts more in keeping with their reading level, and gather other students to help them see how they can transfer the big thinking work we've introduced in the read-aloud to other similar texts.

Finally, we use independent reading as both an assessment and instructional tool. We confer with students to get a sense of how they're thinking in a text on their own and to see who might benefit from small-group support. And we support students right then and there in the conference by offering them specific instruction, which often involves noticing and naming the work we see them doing or reminding them of the work they've done with the whole class or in a small targeted group.

THE POWER OF NOTICING AND NAMING

Combining the components in this way, with small groups and conferences acting as bridges between the whole-class experience and students' independent practice, allows us to consistently reinforce and affirm the work that readers do. What also helps us in that endeavor is the method of noticing and naming, which we first observed in our early days at the Project as we watched Shelley Harwayne and other master teachers confer with student writers, and later read about in more detail in Peter Johnston's *Choice Words*.

No matter what their age, Shelley always approached students in a listening but curious mode. "What are you working on?" she would ask. "What are you thinking about here?" Whatever answer the student provided—be it an articulation of a choice they had made or simply a flustered shrug—Shelley would teach from there. More often than not her teaching consisted of connecting what she'd heard or saw the student doing—i.e., what she noticed—to the work that real writers did—what she named—in a way that elevated and dignified whatever the student was attempting. Thus she'd say to a child hesitating over a word, "So, you're thinking about word choice—just like poets do." Or she'd exclaim to a child she saw furiously drawing, "You're making a picture book— just like Cynthia Rylant."

Hearing their words and their efforts attended to in such a serious way, these children would return to their work with greater awareness and intent—about word choice, for instance, or genre—as well as with a stronger, more confident sense of themselves as writers. The independent thinking, or *agency* as Peter Johnston refers to it, that this fostered is of course another of the capacities cited in the Common Core State Standards' portrait of college- and career-ready students; not insignificantly, it replicates the exact kind of instructional and social interactions associated with effective teaching.

Helping Student Readers Achieve Agency and Independence

Throughout this book, you'll see us noticing and naming the reading work we see ourselves and the teachers and students we work with doing in precise and explicit ways. You'll also see us encouraging students to notice and name what they see themselves doing as they interact with texts. What you won't always see, however, is us teaching a traditional minilesson with a single explicit teaching point at the start of a lesson. This is not because we don't value explicitness; it is, in fact, critical if we're to make the invisible work of reading visible to students. But we heed the words of caution Johnston also provides on the limits of the kind of teaching we tend to equate with explicitness—direct instruction.

> The assumption that just being more explicit will make for better instruction assumes that language is simply a delivery system for information, a literal packaging of knowledge. It is not. Each utterance in a social interaction does much more work. For example, there are hidden costs in telling people things. If a student can figure something out for him- or herself, explicitly providing the information preempts the student's opportunity to build a sense of agency and independence, which, in turn, affects the relationship between teacher and student. (p. 8)

Instead, he says, "The back door is frequently more effective than the front." What we take that to mean here is that, rather than offering an explicit teaching point up front, you'll frequently see us orchestrating scenarios for students that let them experience the work readers do, then naming that work explicitly after they've actually done it. This allows students to actively construct knowledge about the process of reading and the meaning they're making of texts, rather than being passive receptacles of the knowledge we provide. This is important because research has shown that students retain knowledge they construct and uncover better than knowledge they hear or even see demonstrated—and students cannot continue to apply that which they don't retain.

Ultimately, our deepest hope in writing this book is that you don't take our word for it. Rather, we want you to join us in a journey of noticing: noticing your own reading mind at work and noticing your own teaching mind at work. Together, this will have a powerful impact on every student in your class. Hopefully, too, as you read and think and reflect alongside us, you will reexperience the miracle that books can be and the miracle that teaching can be and enter your classroom with a renewed commitment to learn and grow alongside your students.

Chapter One

Stalking the Invisible

What Listening to Students Tells Us
About Reading Instruction

"Goodbye," said the fox. "And now here is my secret,
a very simple secret: It is only with the heart that one can see rightly;
what is essential is invisible to the eye."
"What is essential is invisible to the eye," the little prince repeated
so that he would be sure to remember.

—Antoine de Saint-Exupéry

During a recent election season, we found ourselves walking through a neighborhood in Brooklyn with a colleague and her daughter, Mara, who was in second grade. The shop windows and storefronts were filled with campaign posters for various candidates—bold fonts and bright variations of red-white-and-blue, with the names of the candidates in big letters. Among the posters, though, one was different. This one, also red, white, and blue with a similarly large, bold font, did not spell out the name of an individual candidate but read "Vote or Die." We passed several of these posters as we walked, and soon Mara turned to her mother and asked, "What does that mean?"

We found her question intriguing. We knew that she could "read" each word, literally comprehending "vote," "or," and "die," but clearly when she put the three words together something didn't add up. She must have understood on some level that the phrase did not mean that if you didn't vote you would die and therefore must mean something else, though her question seemed to suggest that that "something else" was beyond her reach, invisible to her in a manner of speaking. Her mother gave a response that every educator will recognize — "What do you think it means?" — and embarked on a conversation with the girl to elicit her thinking. Mara would have none of it. "I dunno," was the gist, and we turned to each other, smiling, "Just like our students, right?"

This set us thinking: If this girl were one of our students and the poster were in one of our classrooms, what would we teach her to do? What skills or strategies would we offer that would allow her to understand the phrase without turning to an adult for an answer? We ran through the comprehension strategies we knew filled the curriculum at Mara's school, as they do many schools around the country. Let's see. She was already monitoring her comprehension since she knew she didn't get it. How about visualizing? No, probably no help. Predicting? Rereading? No again. How about connecting? Maybe a text-to-text connection would help her compare this poster with the others that filled the shop windows, but would that help her understand it? Perhaps inferring. But how? This was probably different than any other inferring she had done. How about activating background knowledge? Hmmm.

We tuned back in to our friend's conversation. It seemed Mara had won the battle, for here was the mother explaining her thinking. After listening for about fifteen seconds, the girl skipped away without comment, perhaps satisfied or perhaps not that interested after all. We would never know.

As we watched her bounce down the street, we turned her question on ourselves — what does it mean? What does it mean about reading instruction that Mara seemed to think there was a single right answer to her question? What does it mean that she seemed to think her mother possessed this answer and she didn't? What does it mean that none of the instruction she's receiving in school seemed likely to help her in this situation, and what does it mean that a ubiquitous teaching method, the think-aloud that her mother eventually undertook, might have accomplished an answer to the question at hand but might also be a contributing factor to the passivity we first observed in her and the disengagement we observed later.

Looking at the Limits of Current Practice

It may be tempting to dismiss this incident as an isolated one—the "text" was clearly above the range of most second graders. To comprehend it required a whole slew of background knowledge, not just about American politics and democracy but also about hyperbole and how campaign posters and advertising work. The reader also had to make a leap from literal to abstract thinking that many educators no doubt consider beyond the normal development of a seven-year-old. Nevertheless, Mara's question to her mother disquieted us precisely because it echoed the way many of our students, most of whom are older than seven, talk and behave as they read—as if meaning consists of a single right answer and resides outside their purview. We began to realize, too, that the text was not that dissimilar from others young students are exposed to. A few months after our walk, for example, we were in a third-grade classroom where the teacher introduced this poem, "The First Day of Spring" by Eve Merriam (2000). While clearly more age-appropriate than the campaign poster, it presents some similar challenges.

The First Day of Spring

The first day of spring
itches
because
an emerald blade of grass
is
pushing out
of
my forehead.
I've become
a unicorn.

Like the "Vote or Die" poster, the poem provides few difficulties at the literal level. The third graders in this class could "comprehend" what it said, and many were amused and delighted by this basic reading of it. Delight and enjoyment are important responses to texts—and, in fact, the teacher had chosen the poem especially because he knew his kids would love it. Yet we sensed that, like the poster, there is more to this poem than first meets the eye, that it means more than the sum of its parts, and that its purpose and message aren't fully visible.

But how, we thought, could we teach these students to access these deeper, invisible levels? We thought again about comprehension strategies. In this classroom a list of these strategies appeared on a chart titled "What Good Readers Do." We had our doubts, just as we had had with Mara, that any of those would have helped. We then thought about lessons from poetry units of study, perhaps something on figurative language, and though this might be a reasonable starting place, we were ultimately troubled by a bigger thought: that for all the time and resources spent on reading instruction, our students ultimately don't know what it means to make meaning. Ellin Keene put her finger on this in her book *To Understand* (2008), where she describes being challenged by a student to explain what she meant by "does it make sense?" Similarly here, we feel challenged to explain—for ourselves and for our students—what we mean by "what does it mean?"

Moving Beyond Engagement to Deeper Thinking About a Text

In part, such a question is a natural outcome of our commitment to reflect on our practice as the best way to learn and improve. Yet it's also a reflection of something else: the nagging sense that many of us in the literacy field sometimes feel that despite the fact that we are doing everything we think we should do—grounding our instruction in research and data, aligning our curricula with standards, making that critical shift in our teaching from being the guardian of knowledge to the facilitator of thinking—something still feels missing. As with the poem and the campaign poster, we sense that our teaching should ultimately add up to more than the sum of its parts, and while that certainly happens sometimes, often it feels hit-or-miss.

Take strategy instruction: When we first began reading about strategy instruction and the research that supported it, we felt our hearts instantly quicken. Here was a way of grounding our teaching in the work that real readers do, just as we framed our writing instruction around the work of real writers. We saw, as well, how it could support that teacherly change we were after, shifting the focus away from us, as authorities on any given text, to the students as practitioners of reading. In fact, when we first began to incorporate strategy instruction in classrooms, it felt like an answer to our prayers. Suddenly students were active and engaged, filling the room up with their voices, joining us in the meeting area with actual excitement. They were asking questions, making predictions, connecting texts to their own lives. They were transacting with the text, which the literary theorist Louise Rosenblatt (1938, 1978) described as the heart and soul of reading.

Yet as that initial exhilaration passed, we began to notice other things. If we weren't careful, all those questions and predictions and connections took over the room. Here we are, for instance, several years ago, reading Eve Bunting's fascinating picture book *Fly Away Home* (1991) to a class of fifth graders, with whom we've been working on connections. On a literal level the book is about a homeless father and son who live in an airport, and when we ask for connections, hands shoot up from children who are eager to share the fact that they've been to an airport before or have seen homeless people on the street. These students are visibly making connections with a sense of accomplishment and zeal, but as they share stories of long lines and plane flights and adventures in food court dining, the book is all but forgotten and we must struggle to rein them in and get back to the text.

Similarly, when we've used *Fly Away Home* to introduce students to questioning, the hands go up in the air: Do the boy and his father ever get to take showers? What happened to the boy's mother? How will the boy go to school? Do school buses even stop at airports? In this instance, the children are definitely curious, and their questions may, indeed, help them understand the innumerable hardships faced by the homeless, which does seem to be one of Eve Bunting's purposes. They are also engaged, which research has proven is connected with student achievement. Yet their questions lead them to speculate about things beyond the realm of the text. And as frequently happens with their connections, as the students speculate on how the mother died or where school buses stop—neither of which is addressed in the book—they move away from the text in a way that actually discourages them from attending to the words on the page.

In a sense, the text has become an occasion or catalyst for students to reconnect with their memories and sense of wonder. There are certainly benefits to such connections—they stoke the students' curiosity about the world around them; they help them value their experience—but they don't necessarily deepen their comprehension, as we thought strategy instruction was meant to do. In fact, the strategies, as we taught them here, seemed to actually get in the way of students digging into the text, taking them off on tangents or what can feel like wild goose chases. And as they pursue those tangents, they are less and less likely to reach any insight about the other ideas or themes that Bunting explores in the book, such as the resilience of families and what's really needed to make a home a home.

Like the meaning of the campaign poster and the poem, these ideas or themes are not directly stated in the text. They are, in effect, invisible and not immediately accessible through strategy use alone. But how could we help students access those invisible levels of texts? We knew we could probably get them there by directing the class to specific passages and asking prompted questions. But how would doing so empower them to reach those deeper levels of thinking on their own? And we feared that all that directing and prompting would bring us right back to a teacher-centered classroom that we had tried so hard to move away from. And so we experimented. We tried to do more think-alouds to make the work our minds were doing as we navigated a text more visible, and we added more interactive prompts, such as putting yourself in a character's shoes, which were aimed at helping students stick closer to the text. For a few children this did, indeed, work, yet too often we encountered variations on the following:

We are in a sixth-grade classroom doing a read-aloud of *Ella Enchanted* by Gail Carson Levine (1997), an original take on the story of Cinderella that the class is studying as part of their unit on fairy tales. In this day's chapter, Ella is riding in a carriage with her two wicked stepsisters, who have demanded that Ella give them the necklace that her mother gave to her as a child. Ella is under a spell of obedience and so must comply with such a request. But before she does, we stop and ask the students to imagine themselves in Ella's shoes, then turn and talk to a partner about what they think she should do.

We are hoping this prompt will act as an inroad for the students to the book's deeper meaning, enabling them to better understand and appreciate the complexity of Ella's situation. But when we hunker down to listen to two students, what we hear gives us pause. Jamal is telling his partner, Lisette, that he wouldn't give the necklace away. "Nope," he says, crossing his arms in defiance. "I don't care what those stepsisters say, I simply wouldn't do it." Lisette says nothing and keeps her head down until we prod her to share, and in a voice that's barely a whisper she says that she would just try to stay quiet in the hopes that the stepsisters would ignore or forget her.

On the one hand, both children have done precisely what Rosenblatt says readers do: They have brought "to the work personality traits, memories of past events, present needs and preoccupations, a particular mood of the moment, and a particular physical condition" (pp. 30–31). Yet each, in effect, superimposed their own personality and agenda on Ella in a way that hinders, rather than advances, their understanding of both her predicament and her nature as a character. They have responded and, in a certain sense, transacted. But they have failed to do what Rosenblatt, as paraphrased here by Robert Probst in his book, *Response & Analysis* (2004), also says a reader must do: ". . . accommodate herself to the text. She must be in some ways guided, or she is fantasizing rather than reading" (p. 17).

Without doing this, Jamal and Lisette run the risk of missing whatever Gail Carson Levine had hoped her readers would consider. And they furthermore miss the ultimate benefits of transacting with the text: the opportunity and ability to gain "access to insights, experiences and perceptions that would otherwise lie beyond [their] reach, thus allowing them to reformulate [their] own consciousness" (p. 24). In Jamal's case this might mean seeing a glimmer of the limits of defiance as a way of dealing with obligations, and perhaps in Lisette's, the beginning of a vision of positive self-assertion. Yet instead of this, their transactions and responses ended right where they started, with what they already knew.

Envisioning Instruction That Creates Ability Through Effort

Some might attribute Jamal and Lisette's inability to more deeply engage or understand the text to their age and stage of development, just as we were ready to do with our second-grade friend Mara and the campaign poster. Sixth graders, they could argue, are not always able to see beyond their own reality in a way that might let them fully appreciate the complexities of Ella's situation—let alone consider how that understanding might inform their own behavior. Perhaps such work is the province of older students, who may be more developmentally ready to consider another person's perspective and reflect on themselves. Yet we often see and hear children even younger than Jamal and Lisette interact with a text in this way. A student will make an insightful connection that we'll share with the rest of the class. Another will reveal deep thinking in a conference, like a fourth-grade student we spoke with as she was reading one of the *Warriors* books by Erin Hunter (2007):

Dorothy: So what are you thinking as you read this page?

Isabella: Well, I'm imagining how Brambleclaw is feeling.

Dorothy: How is he feeling?

Isabella: Confused.

Dorothy: Confused, hmm. Are you confused or is the character confused?

Isabella: No, I'm not confused. The author tells the reader the information, but the character doesn't know it. It makes me wish that I could talk to him and tell him what I think he should do.

Dorothy: Can you show me where you wanted to do that?

Isabella: This line. [She points to the following line: *To save himself, to save Firestar and Thunderclan, there was only one thing he could do* (p. 298).]

Dorothy: So what did you want to say to Brambleclaw when you read that line?

Isabella: "Don't trust him!"

Dorothy: Why did you want to say that?

Isabella: Well, from this line [she points to an earlier line, *"Because you're weak," Hawkfrost taunted him. "You care more for kin than for power. But I don't"* (p. 298).]–I thought about the word power. All Hawkfrost cares about is power. He is just like his father, Tigerstar, who is evil. And this word, *taunted*. It makes me think that Hawkfrost doesn't really care for Brambleclaw even though Hawkfrost is Brambleclaw's brother. He shouldn't trust anybody now, not even his own brother.

This student is accommodating herself to the text precisely as Rosenblatt says she must do in order to truly transact. She is staying very close to the page, considering the meaning of individual words and bringing her full knowledge of each character to the scene, along with her own understanding about people, in order to interpret it. And she furthermore demonstrates a deep understanding that the author has crafted the story in a way that allows the reader to understand more than the character does, and she keeps on reading in part to discover if the character will eventually see what the author has already made clear to her— that Brambleclaw should not trust Hawkfrost.

But what supports such sophisticated thinking? Has this student benefited from instruction that's given her a clear vision and model? Is she one of those students who "got" our think-alouds or latched onto the concept of putting herself in a character's shoes? Or does she have some kind of special aptitude or disposition for penetrating thought? Given how infrequently we see or hear this level of thinking in classrooms, we might conclude that it is the latter and that, unlike Lisette and Jamal, this student has some innate ability that allows her to read deeply. But does this mean that students like Lisette and Jamal, who may not have any specialized aptitude, can't *learn* to take on this kind of thinking?

Lauren Resnik tackles this question head on in her article "From Aptitude to Effort: A New Foundation in Our Schools" (1995), where she suggests that, in all sorts of implicit and explicit ways, schools are often aptitude-oriented. We measure IQs, we grade on a curve, we differentiate curricula according to ability, lowering our expectations for students who do not possess natural strengths. Such practices, she writes, "are expressions of a belief in the importance of aptitude . . . [and] their routine, largely unquestioned use continues to create evidence that confirms aptitude-based thinking." But what would happen, she goes on to ask, if "[e]ducational institutions could be built around the alternative assumption that effort actually creates ability. . . . What would such a system look like? How might it work?"

What *would* such a system look like? And what, exactly, would the expert instruction and clear expectations that Resnik says are necessary components of an effort-based system consist of in a literacy classroom? These are the very questions we found ourselves asking. And they are the very questions we hope to answer over the course of the book as we look at the kinds of instruction and support we believe every student needs to read deeply, not just those who, whether through intellectual or cultural advantage, arrive in our classrooms already poised to get it. In subsequent chapters, we'll explore precisely what such instruction can look and sound like through actual classroom case histories. But first we share some of the conclusions and underlying beliefs we reached as we continued to question and reflect on our practice and our classroom experience.

Reframing Strategies as Tools, Not Products

As we pondered what was happening with our strategy instruction, we came to several conclusions. The first was the discomfiting realization that while we were grounding our lessons in real literature—books that Ralph Peterson and Maryann Eeds, the authors of the now classic *Grand Conversations: Literature Groups in Action* (2007), describe as those "written by authors who know how to unlock the world with words and to open our eyes and our hearts" (p. 1)—we were, in effect, using those books to practice strategies in isolation. Thus, we asked students to make connections or predictions, ask questions, and visualize without explicitly asking—or expecting—them to think about whether those strategies were opening their eyes and hearts to matters they might not have seen otherwise. It was as if we were piano teachers who used the piano to have our students practice scales instead of playing full pieces of music, which required not only a knowledge of notes but an ability to read the textual cues—the crescendo and decrescendo marks, the notations for staccato and legato—needed for interpretation.

Of course, in our defense, we did seize those moments when a student's connection or question held a nugget of insight, which we brought back to the text. That was because we were, in fact, assessing their responses in our heads, drawing on what we knew about texts and our own experience as readers to zoom in on a response that seemed meaningful, while tactfully skipping the rest. But we never made that process visible to our students, nor did we share what we knew as readers that enabled us to recognize which responses were plumbing deep and which were staying on the surface in a way that might empower the students to focus on the former, not the latter.

As it was, most of the students' connections stayed on that surface level. On hearing Cynthia Rylant's story "Spaghetti" (1985), for instance, in which a boy finds a stray kitten, many students shared stories about their own encounters with strays; while the picture book *Something Beautiful* by Sharon Dennis Wyeth (1998), about a girl who lives in a building where someone has written the word "Die" on the front door, sparked lots of connections about the graffiti students had seen near their homes. These connections might help students visualize, but they didn't always yield the "aha" moments attached to deeper thinking. Similarly, students' predictions often stayed on the surface level of plot; they predicted what would happen next, not what the text might be "about" in a deeper or more thematic way.

This led us to the conclusion that some of the so-called comprehension strategies—especially visualizing, predicting, connecting, and questioning—seemed aimed more at helping students develop the habits of active and engaged readers rather than to specifically help them comprehend more than they might have if they had not applied the strategy. To push students further, beyond the surface levels that typical strategy instruction often yielded, we would need to come up with other ways of thinking and talking about strategies that were more clearly tied to demonstrable ends that the students could assess for themselves. We would need, in effect, to find strategies for the strategies to ensure they were used as meaning-making tools, not as end products in and of themselves. If not, we feared that insight and understanding risked becoming little more than incidental by-products of wholesale strategy practice, not the explicitly intended goal for every child in the room.

We also realized that some of the strategies that did seem more specifically linked to meaning, such as inferring and determining the main idea, were, in fact, complicated skills, requiring the application of a variety of strategies. Kylene Beers states this, as well, describing in her book, *When Kids Can't Read* (2002), how inferring is really a sophisticated skill masquerading as a strategy. She goes on to explain how those terms differ through the useful analogy of bicycle riding. "Remember learning to ride with no hands?" she writes. "That's a skill; it's the end product of a lot of practice. Getting to that skill, you might need a strategy such as learning to balance the bike by shifting your weight, not by maneuvering the handlebars. The strategy takes you to the skill" (p. 45).

While we are learning, we often need to keep strategies front and center in our mind. In Beers' example, that means making a conscientious effort to balance a bicycle by shifting our body weight, not relying on the handlebars. Once we master a skill, though, like riding with no hands, we no longer need to think so deliberately about the strategy. Shifting our weight becomes second nature; we do it without visible effort. In fact, it becomes so automatic that we barely remember how we once had to struggle and remind ourselves constantly, in a deliberate way, to apply the strategy.

The same is true with reading. As proficient readers reading a text within our comfort zone, we've internalized so completely the thinking processes involved in making meaning that we're barely aware of them. We read the words and get the meaning instantly, as do a few of our students. Some children, through aptitude or that special synergy that can happen between a reader and a certain text, immediately seem to "get it," while others remain lost—even when they are reading a book in their comfort zone. We believed that we could help those children build the ability to "get it" through effort, provided we parse those complex skills into more explicit strategies and steps. But where, we wondered, would we find those strategies?

Drawing on What We Do as Readers to Make Our Instruction More Explicit

There are, indeed, some professional texts, like Beers' book, that offer useful pointers. Ultimately, however, we discovered that if we attended to our own reading process, carefully thinking about what it was we did, automatically and often invisibly as readers, in order to make meaning, we could help students, offering them more precise and concrete strategies for skills they hadn't yet mastered. We'll delve into this in more depth throughout the rest of the book, but to illustrate it now, let's visit a fifth-grade special ed classroom in New York City's Staten Island where many students struggled to identify character traits, something they will need to do both to pass the state's high-stakes ELA test and meet the then current New York State Standards.

To help the students, their teacher had provided the class with a graphic organizer that consisted of a large box at the top of the page, in which the children were instructed to name a trait for a particular character, then place the evidence they found in the text to support their thinking in three smaller boxes that radiated out from the larger trait box. The students had practiced this enough to become familiar with the concept of supporting their thinking with evidence, but their thinking was not terribly perceptive, with most of the students identifying characters as either "nice" or "not nice."

Seeing this initially as a problem of vocabulary, we had helped create a list of more precise descriptive words—*determined, courageous, clever*, and the like—which the teacher had hung prominently on the wall. And while this did seem to help a little, students would often look at the chart and seemingly choose words at random, looking at us for confirmation with a questioning lilt in their voice. This made us worry that, despite our best intentions, we were back where we started, as the gatekeeper of content, giving students our thinking and our words, not helping them find their own. And so we tried to peer into our minds to unearth the work we did so automatically as readers we were barely aware of it. Perhaps if we could name that work, clearly and concisely, these students might be able to do it on their own in a way that felt more empowering.

What we realized was that, as readers, we paid attention to the details the author had given us about the character and from there inferred what kind of person that character was—i.e., what is often called their traits. Furthermore, we knew to do that because we were aware that the author chose those details for the express purpose of giving us a feel for the character. But the graphic organizer kept all that work invisible. It asked kids to use what we could call deductive or top-down thinking—that is, to start off with an idea and then see if they could support it with evidence. But it gave them no strategies for coming up with the idea in the first place, leaving students to succeed or not according to whatever ability or experience they already brought to the task. Instead we thought we needed to teach these students to think inductively, using details from the texts to construct an idea from the bottom-up. Focusing on particular kinds of details would be, in effect, a strategy for the skill of inferring a deeper understanding about a character.

With this in mind, we gathered three of the most struggling students, Desmond, Edgar, and Sharif, and asked them to read the first few pages of *A Pony Named Shawney*, a short chapter book by Mary Small (1997) about a paraplegic boy named Scott who encounters a pony that, according to the blurb on the back of the book, "would change his life forever." When the students had finished reading the passage, we asked them how they'd describe Scott's character. Immediately all three boys said, "Nice," with Sharif, familiar with the drill, adding, "because it says he feeds the pony."

"That does make him sound nice, but are there any other words you'd use to describe Scott?" we asked. At this point, the boys all looked at the word wall.

"Confident?" Desmond said, his voice belying his own lack of confidence in his offering.

"Okay," we said, "Let's try something different. I want to share with you something that I do as a reader. When I'm reading, I pay really close attention to the details the author gives me about what a character is doing, because I know that the author has carefully chosen those details to give me a feel for the kind of person that character is. I think that that might work for you, too. So let's read the end of this section again, paying really close attention to what the author is telling us Scott does, and then let's think about what kind of person might do those kinds of things."

And so the students returned to the text, rereading the following passage with the specific goal of attending to what Mary Small tells us Scott does:

> *Scott was unable to walk. Often people felt sorry for him, but mostly he didn't mind so much. He had never known what it felt like to be able to walk. Scott could just manage to get around on a pair of crutches, but very slowly. He spent most of his time in his wheelchair. It was nearly as good as a car! He could go almost anywhere in it, as long as he avoided loose stones, curbs, and steps. He had lost count of how many times the wheelchair had run away with him, helter-skelter, and tipped him out onto the ground. But except for scratches and bruises, he was never hurt.*
>
> *"The boy's made of rubber," his father said. "He'll never learn to be careful enough. All the same he's got plenty of guts." (pp. 5–6)*

After a brief discussion of the word *helter-skelter*, the students said that Scott goes all over the place in his wheelchair, even though he often loses control of it and winds up falling on the ground.

"Okay, that's what the author is telling us Scott does. Now our job as readers is to think about what kind of person would do that?"

"I think you'd gotta be brave to do that," Desmond said.

"That's not brave, that's crazy," Edgar countered. "He sounds pretty crazy to me."

"Well, I think he's a daredevil," said Sharif, using a word that neither Desmond nor Edgar had heard of before—and that did not appear on the word wall. He explained what the word meant by describing someone he'd seen on TV who sounded to us like Evel Knievel, riding a motorcycle over a line of cars. After batting these words back and forth, the boys decided that a daredevil was someone who was both crazy and brave. And all three agreed that that described Scott perfectly.

"Yeah, look what his father says," Edgar added, pointing to the end of the passage. "He's not careful but he has guts. That's like a daredevil, too."

"And he keeps on feeding the pony," Desmond said, referring to an earlier section, "even though his mom says not to go near it because it could bite or kick."

"Wow," we said, bringing the group to a close. "Do you know what you just did? Not only did you get a much deeper understanding of Scott by paying attention to what the author told us he did, you connected what you were learning from those details to what the author tells us other people thought and said about Scott. That's just what readers do to get a handle on what kind of person a character is. They connect all these details to come up with an understanding of something the author doesn't come right out and say."

Considering the Instructional Implications

Teachers and students left the classroom that day feeling satisfied and successful. Desmond, Edgar, and Sharif recognized that by reading more closely and sharing their thoughts, they'd arrived at an understanding of Scott that was more insightful and astute than their original sense of him as "nice." And we felt we'd accomplished what we set out to do: to offer a strategy—i.e., thinking about what specific details suggest about a character in general—that was precise and explicit enough for students to fully own the thinking and clearly see how applying the strategy led to deeper meaning and, in turn, a new sense of confidence and pride in their ability as readers.

As we contemplated our next steps, we made a note to confer with each student during independent reading to see how they transferred the thinking they'd done together to their own chosen books. We knew that we might need to remind them of what they had done as readers and ask them to keep practicing that thinking deliberately until it became second nature. We also wanted to connect the work they'd done to a skill they'd struggled with for years: inferring. Inferring was something that none of the boys felt particularly adept at. They knew conceptually what it meant, but had no reliable understanding of when, how, and why to do it. Yet, with precise scaffolding and instruction, that's exactly the work they did so successfully with *A Pony Named Shawney*. They inferred what kind of person Scott was from the details the author provided. Naming that work as inferring for them, now that they'd experienced firsthand what that thinking felt and sounded like, would be far more powerful and more lasting, we felt, than if we had brought up the term earlier. Now they had something to attach it to. Now they were ready to hear it.

Finally, we noted how much more effective this "strategy" was than the ones we'd been teaching. Had we asked for connections, we thought it was likely that one boy would recall his use of crutches, another his experience with a wheelchair. And while pushing for the feelings attached to those connections might lead to a deeper appreciation of the challenges all paraplegics faced, we doubt it would have yielded the insight the students had about this particular character. Sharif, of course, did make a connection, as he recalled the television show with the daredevil motorcycle driver, but the connection was a direct result of his contemplating what kind of person would do the things Scott did, not because of a general call for connections.

When and how readers make useful connections was something we'd continue pondering, along with several other questions the group work had raised. Could we, for example, help those same students construct an understanding of a theme of an entire text the way we'd help them construct an initial understanding of a single character, by giving them explicit, concrete strategies based on the work readers do? Did they have any idea of why it was important to think about characters—or themes, for that matter—beyond the ability to meet a standard or answer a question on a test? Did they know that, having reached this understanding, they'd need to keep reading attentively to see how Scott developed over time, knowing that in books, just as in life, people change and learn and grow—just as, through effort, they had changed here from students who couldn't to those who could? And if they didn't, was it because we'd failed to make that visible as well? We feared that the answer to this last question was yes. But unlike the fox in *The Little Prince*, whom we quoted at the beginning of this chapter, we believed that if we looked into our hearts to "see" what was most essential about reading, we could make that essential heart of reading visible to the eyes of the teachers and students we worked with, to our readers, and to ourselves.

In the following chapter we share what we discovered as we peered into our hearts to explore what was essential about reading, beginning with that thorny question: What do we mean by making meaning? We'll also invite you to read a text along with us, as we notice and name the invisible work that proficient readers do, in a way that will ultimately allow us as teachers to design authentic, meaningful instruction for every child in the room.

Chapter Two

What We Mean by Meaning Making

Noticing and Naming What We Do as Readers

I believe in the power and mystery of naming things. Language has the capacity to transform our cells, rearrange our learned patterns of behavior, and redirect our thinking. I believe in naming what's right in front of us because that is often what is most invisible.

—Eve Ensler

So what exactly do we mean by making meaning? When we first asked ourselves that question and posed it to teachers we worked with, we felt like we'd opened a can of worms. Was meaning making the same as comprehending? Was it the main idea? Was it the author's purpose or message? And what about that word, *theme*, familiar to us from English classes, and those other words that often lurk in the air and occasionally appear in rubrics and standards, words like *interpretation, analysis,* and *deeper understanding*? Were they all interchangeable? Did they mean the same thing? Or did they each mean something different? And did it really matter anyway as long as kids were reading?

We believe it does matter, if we think that by reading we mean more than word calling or glancing over the words on a page the way a couch potato watches TV. We believe it matters, too, if we're committed to making the work of reading more visible to every student, in every room, regardless of aptitude, age, or experience. We think, for instance, of Lisette and Jamal, our two sixth graders who seemed unable to put themselves in Ella's enchanted shoes. We're convinced they would benefit from the kind of strategy instruction we offered to Desmond, Edgar, and Sharif, the fifth graders from Staten Island, instruction that anchored them more deeply in the text and securely tied the means to a visible end. But they also might need a clearer vision and a taste of those ends—not just what it sounds like to understand a character but how reading can inform and affect our lives, how it can open our minds and our hearts—in order to know more precisely what to work toward and be motivated to do so. Yet if we're unable to answer these questions for ourselves, how will we ever be able to offer a vision to children like Lisette and Jamal?

To define those terms, we could, of course, turn to a dictionary or Bloom's Taxonomy. We could consult professional books that also address such questions. We believe, however, that the most effective way of tackling these questions is to actually read: to read attending to what we do as readers, noticing and naming and making visible the work we routinely and invisibly do. Doing so, we're convinced, can deepen and strengthen our instruction more than any compendium of tips or even research-based theories, because it authentically grounds our teaching in our life as readers. And so we invite you to read along with us as we replicate here a workshop we've facilitated with teachers where we try to notice and name the work they're doing in a way that illuminates not only what we mean by meaning, but how and why we read.

Connecting with Ourselves as Readers: An Interactive Experience

To begin, we ask that you first read the following and try to take stock of what's going through your mind:

Cupcakes

Brownies

Boy scouts

Alligator

Vodka

Crayon

Baseball

Pies

Meatloaf

Kahlua

Guitar

Belt

Soccer

Stew

Hand

Bread

Hairbrush

Scotch

If you are like any of the dozens of teachers we've read this with, you probably attempted to assign some meaning to the words by trying to somehow categorize them or discern some pattern in their order. You may have even interpreted this "text," seeing it as "a mother's to-do list," "things you take on a picnic," or "an alcoholic's nightmare," as some of our workshop participants have. Or you may simply have scratched your head, not sure what to make of it.

Now let's look at the following poem by Susan Marie Scavo (1999), from which the above words were taken. We ask that you try to read it twice, attending to what you're thinking and feeling and to what in the text is contributing to or triggering those thoughts and feelings.

Food. Music. Memory.

She says: Cupcakes. Brownies. Pies. She says:
Remember this. Bread. Stew. Sauce. She says:
All that time. She says: Singing. All I taught
you. She says: Crayon, Alligator. Boy Scouts.
She says: Baseball. Soccer. Track. She says:
I was there. Remember?

I say: Shouting. Silence. Shouting. I say:
Remember this: Scotch. Vodka. Kahlua. I say:
Cupcake. Meatloaf. Sauce. I say: Singing. All
you would not tell me. I say: Crayon. Dancing.
Guitar. I say: Belt. Hairbrush. Hand. I say:
I was there. Remember?

Frequently we hear a collective "Oh!" as teachers move from the list to the poem. When we ask them to articulate what's behind the "Oh!," we usually hear variations on the statement, "Now the words make sense!" In effect, the "Oh!" is the sound of making meaning, of realizing how all the words add up to more than the sum of their parts to create an emotional or intellectual impact on the reader. Presenting the list first drives that point home. It also reveals some critical things that we know about texts that we don't always share with our students, things that we do so automatically, we're barely aware of them.

What Readers Expect from Texts

Whether you tried to interpret the words that were taken out of context or not, you viewed the list, in effect, as a text and brought to it the assumption that the details the author provided carried some significance that you tried to discern. Put another way, you expected those details to mean something, and you knew that one of your main jobs as a reader was to consider the significance of those details, both individually and in relation to the whole, by constantly asking yourself the question: What does that mean? Without the guiding hand of an author, however, who had carefully chosen and arranged those details for a particular purpose, you couldn't quite do that successfully.

On the one hand this may seem obvious, but it runs counter to some of what we say to our students. As teachers, we sometimes tell our students to focus on the main idea of a text and not get lost in the details. The details, we convey, can be a distraction; they are interesting, perhaps, but not the real crux, useful as evidence or for visualizing, but dispensable after that. As readers, however, we know that details are the building blocks and lifeblood of texts, and we attend to them closely, whether we're fully conscious of this or not, contemplating their significance in a way that ultimately allows us to make meaning of what we've read.

What Readers Do to Make Meaning

With a poem like "Food. Music. Memory.," this happens rather quickly. We read the poem and feel its impact almost immediately, and especially if we're in a setting like a workshop where we're asked to share our thoughts, we're able to articulate what we think the poem is "about." One teacher, for instance, said the poem was "clearly" about a mother and daughter who have two different perspectives of a childhood; others disagreed and read the two stanzas as belonging to a mother and son or possibly to siblings; yet another thought the poem was about two internal voices warring with each other.

These are, in effect, interpretations—none of them "right," none of them "wrong," but all of them growing out of clues gathered from the text. Many children, however, are unable to do this with the lightning-flash speed that we do; in fact, many middle school students who we've looked at this poem with are as initially puzzled by it as we were by the list. They don't automatically see the connection between the details, nor their significance. To them, the words and their arrangement seem random or reportorial, an objective laundry list of facts that holds none of the emotional heft and resonance that we felt.

So how do we help those students make some age-appropriate meaning of a text like this (something, perhaps, along the line of "grown-ups never get it")? To do so, we believe we must slow down our thinking and look more closely at how we moved from reading the words to making sense of them, bringing into the light of day what usually stays invisible. When we've done this with teachers, we've noticed several things. Virtually all readers attend to the pronouns—the "She" of the first stanza and the "I" of the second—and the stanzas themselves that separate those pronouns. And most note a similarity in the kinds of details found in the two stanzas, with the cupcakes, the crayons, the boy scouts, and sports of the first stanza associated with a child or childhood, while the scotch and the vodka of the second evoke a grown-up or adulthood. Most also take note of the many other patterns established—the repetition of words and punctuation and syntactical structures—or consider specific words and the order in which those words were written in order to infer some meaning. "Belt. Hairbrush. Hand" for instance, conveys a different meaning than those words in isolation might, with many readers inferring that these details refer to some history of physical abuse. Likewise, the word "Sauce" in the second stanza takes on a different connotation for some readers than it does in the first because it follows the line, "Scotch. Vodka. Kahlua."

Having attended to all of these parts of the poem—and coming to it with the premise that these parts have been deliberately chosen and arranged by the author for some discernible purpose—readers then interpret what they've comprehended from the parts as a way of making sense of the whole. For some, the poem seems to speak to them directly; the words are an expression of what they've felt themselves, a reflection of their own experience so profound it's as if the writer has seen into their heart and placed it, still beating, on the page. Those readers will bring that sense of recognition to their interpretation, often seeing the "I" in the poem as themselves. Thus, if they're women they'll most likely interpret the "I" as a daughter or a sister; if men, they'll see it as a son. Readers who don't feel their own experience mirrored in the poem in quite that self-reflecting way do additional work. Some might notice, for example, that the writer is a woman and so interpret the "I" as female; others might note the reference to boy scouts and interpret the "I" as male.

Either way, what's important to point out here is the fact that, like Desmond, Edgar, and Sharif's understanding about the character in A Pony Named Shawney, all these interpretations are constructed bottom-up, or inductively, from the details of the text. They'll also be used as evidence as we try to explain to others why we see the poem the way that we do, but that comes after we've used them to build our understanding in the first place. This is a vital step that is all too often missing from our classroom instruction, especially with the kind of step-by-step explicitness and concreteness that some students need and we provide throughout the rest of the book.

The Role of Talk in Meaning Making: A Process of Drafting and Revising

Once the participants in our workshop have had the opportunity to read the poem twice, attending to both the parts and the whole, what they think it's "about" and why, we ask everyone to share their thinking. What happens then is what may have happened to you as you read some of the above-noted interpretations: You reconsidered your own take on the poem, returning to it, on the page or in your mind, to reread and rethink it yet again. You may have, for example, been struck by something someone else had seen that you hadn't considered before: the possibility that the "I" was a different gender than you'd imagined or that it could be one half of a self arguing with its other half. Or you might have felt your own take affirmed by other people's similar reading. Either way, you may have returned to the poem with a new admiration for the work of the poet and your fellow readers, feeling both the text and your own mind enlarged as you reread it with a new set of eyes.

If so, you did what the workshop participants did: You revised your initial understanding of the poem in light of new information, as if that first under-standing was a draft. This is what we do as readers: We adjust and deepen our thinking about a text as we encounter new details and/or other people's thoughts—though to do so we must be flexible and willing to entertain a range of ideas before setting our own thinking in stone. We must also be willing to offer up thoughts when they're still a work-in-progress, when our ideas are tentative and not yet fully formed, which is hard for children who have come to believe that there's always a right or wrong answer. Over the years we've had the privilege of working in many classrooms where children do not silence themselves out of fear of evaluation. These are classrooms where children's voices and thoughts are honored and celebrated by teachers who have created environments where students are comfortable taking risks. Yet as Sheridan Blau points out in *The Literature Workshop* (2003), "most students have never had the opportunity to learn that reading, like writing, is a process of making meaning . . . that is frequently accompanied by false starts and faulty visions requiring frequent and messy reconstruction and revision" (p. 31). And if they haven't learned it, we believe it's because we haven't explicitly taught it.

The false starts and messiness are compounded even more when we read a text that's longer than Scavo's poem, a text that unfolds over several to hundreds of pages and can't be digested all at once. The process then is a little more like what happened when we moved from the list to the poem: We had an initial tentative take—a first-draft understanding, if you will—on what the words on the list might connote, but it was only as we kept on reading that the significance of those details revealed themselves fully. And so we had to revise. The teacher who, on encountering the details for the first time, thought they might be picnic provisions abandoned that line of thinking entirely when she came to the poem, seeing it as a false start; while the teacher who initially interpreted those same details as "an alcoholic's nightmare" might build on that idea, modifying and expanding it rather than completely rejecting it. This doesn't mean that the first teacher got it "wrong" while the second got it "right," only that both were engaged in the same process of drafting and revising.

We'll explore in more detail what this process looks like in longer narrative texts, and how to explicitly teach it to students, starting with the next chapter; but first we return to the workshop one last time to experience our final meaning-making step.

Contemplating What Our Minds and Hearts Were Opened To

"Why are we reading," writer Annie Dillard (1989) asks, "if not in hope of beauty laid bare, life heightened, and its deepest mystery probed?" (p. 72). Why, indeed, especially when life presents us and our students with so many other diversions and distractions? If you believe, as we do, that reading can open our minds and our hearts and help us probe life's deepest mysteries, it follows suit that we must ask ourselves what our minds and hearts were opened to and what mysteries were probed through our reading. We direct the teachers in our workshops to consider this very question, asking them how the poem spoke to them and what, if any, insight, affirmation, or relevance it offered them as readers.

The poem speaks to readers in many different ways—as it may have spoken uniquely to you—and as the teachers talk in small groups, we overhear many stories. There are stories of alcoholism and physical abuse—"This is what it was like for me," "I grew up never knowing what mood would hit when—the cupcake or the belt." One woman in a group said, "I was there, too," and we all turned our eyes back to the last line in the poem with a fresh "Oh."

There are other stories, too, less specifically tied to the references to alcohol and abuse and more related to the idea of perspective or perception that the poet seems to be showing us. The poem speaks to these readers as well: "My sister and I have completely different takes on our childhood," one teacher said.

"Yeah," said another, pointing to one of the mysteries he thought the poem probed, "there's times when you can't believe that two people were both at the same event." One teacher said, "It's important for everyone to think about how others might see a situation"; while another added on, "It's especially important for teachers to think about that—the perspective of our students." The woman who interpreted the poem as being about an internal voice spoke up: "This helps me see that one side is never going to win. There will always be an argument going on in my head. I just have to accept that." And another acknowledged that woman's contribution to what she was taking away with her: "Both you and the poem are making me realize that I need to watch out for those times when I justify or rationalize my behavior. I do that sometimes, I rewrite my own history, leaving certain parts out, and I'm not sure that's a good thing to do."

What Readers Know About How Texts Work

In one way or another, all these readers recognized that the poem was "about" more than its particulars—that is, more than just the "she" who drank Kahlua and the "I" who played the guitar. They understood that, through these particulars, the poem was addressing something more universal: the way two people sharing the same experience never quite see the same thing; the damage parents can inflict on a child; the danger of rationalizing. In this way they seemed to instinctively know that the text was in and of itself a kind of metaphor, that its details stood for something. Just as individual details became stand-ins for ideas—Kahlua for alcoholism, for example, or cupcakes for a loving home—so the whole text put together became a stand-in for larger ideas.

Readers seem to know that this is how texts operate to the point where we expect significance from the first word, as we attempted to highlight in our workshop through the use of the list. Whether they consciously realized it or not, they knew about texts what poet Diane Ackerman (1991) knows when she says,

> . . . the subject of a poem [isn't] an end in itself. What it usually is is an occasion, catalyst, or tripwire that permits the poet to reach into herself and haul up whatever nugget of the human condition distracts her at the moment. (p. 207)

Though she is writing about poetry, this understanding can also be applied to narrative texts, as we will explore in detail later in this book. Yet it is this understanding—about how texts operate and how readers move from the particular to the universal, from interpretation, if we want to use academic terms, to theme—that frequently remains invisible, both in our minds as we read and in much of our teaching. Unless we make this knowledge and process visible for our students, many will be unable to engage in evaluation, without which the cycle of meaning making is incomplete. More critically, students will miss out on one of the most valuable benefits of reading, which writer Milan Kundera (2007) explains this way:

> Every reader, as he reads, is actually the reader of himself. The writer's work is only a kind of optical instrument he provides the reader so he can discern what he might never have seen without the book. The reader's recognition in himself of what the book says is the proof of the book's truth. (p. 96)

The teachers in the workshop recognized both the truth in the poem and in Kundera's words. They recognized additionally how they were able to formulate multiple and individual interpretations precisely because they accommodated themselves to the text in the first place, as Robert Probst reminds us that readers need to do. From the smallest pieces of texts—its words, punctuation marks, and structures—they drafted and revised their thinking. They connected all the small pieces together, discovering patterns, inferring and interpreting, talking with each and reconsidering the small pieces, pulling them all together into a whole as they continued constructing understandings.

And so the workshop concluded and everyone returned to their lives—as teachers, as parents, as daughters and sons, as learners and as readers. In a sense we left the text behind, but we also carried it with us. We thought about it as we picked up the phone and called our mother and sister; we considered it as we sat around the dinner table with our children; we remembered it as we walked into our classrooms and wondered anew about how our students were perceiving all that goes on there. For this is what happens when we read deeply: The text becomes part of our experience. We learn and grow from our reading and recognize that we construct understandings not only of a text, but of ourselves and the world around us.

Naming the Strands of Thinking Involved in Reading: Comprehension, Understanding, and Evaluation

We've asked you to connect with yourself as a reader before offering any critical framework or theory because we believe it's important to have that firsthand experience as a reader in your mind before taking on outside knowledge. It is, in effect, what we did with Desmond, Edgar, and Sharif—not introducing the technical term "inferring" until they'd gotten a feel for the thinking, believing that the word would make more sense afterward, not beforehand. Now, though, in our attempt to make the thinking involved in meaning making more explicit, we draw on the work of other educators and scholars to help name the parts of the process, or what we might call the levels or the strands involved in the thinking work of reading. In particular, we look at the work of Robert Scholes who, in his seminal work *Textual Power: Literary Theory and the Teaching of English* (1985), parsed what he called "textual competence"—i.e., the skills needed to be an accomplished reader—into three distinct, but interrelated, modes of thinking: reading, interpretation, and criticism. We've adapted this framework in ways that we hope untangle the terms we began the chapter with, seeing making meaning as comprising three strands—comprehension, under-standing, and evaluation, which we define as follows.

By comprehension we mean the literal and inferential sense readers make of a text on a line-by-line and page-by-page basis. In "Food. Music. Memory.," for instance, we did the work of comprehension as we recognized the literal presence of two voices through the pronouns "She" and "I" and the structure of the two stanzas, and we assigned some significance to clusters of details, such as "Belt. Hairbrush. Hand," through inferring. Similarly, Desmond, Edgar, and Sharif were engaged in comprehension as they clarified the word *helter-skelter* in order to make literal sense of what the author had written, then considered what else she was telegraphing about the character through those details by inferring.

Particularly when it involves inferring, comprehension is complicated work, but it's not the only work readers engage in. In fact, in a sense, it's the floor, not the ceiling, of meaning making. Readers take what they comprehend line-by-line and use that to construct an understanding of the bigger messages, concerns, or themes of the text. Understanding involves inferring on a larger scale, as readers recognize patterns and motifs, changes and variations. In a sense, readers connect the dots of their line-by-line, page-by-page comprehension in order to help them see a bigger picture that may not have been apparent before.

With Scavo's poem, we shifted quite quickly from comprehension to understanding as we shared our interpretations of the relationship between the two characters, what we thought had happened between them and why, and how we thought the poem, in a more general way, seemed to be thematically exploring the subjectivity of perception, among other things. We were able to do so with relative ease because the poem was short and within our comfort zone—i.e., not too difficult for us to comprehend—though, as you saw, there were many interpretations, which prompted us to return to the poem to revise and deepen our thinking. Desmond, Edgar, and Sharif, however, hadn't yet embarked on understanding, partly because they were at the very beginning of a longer narrative work. Understanding that text would in some way entail attending to how the character of Scott developed over time, and perhaps by thinking about whether that daredevil trait they'd comprehended in the passage helped or hindered him as he encountered whatever twists and turns the author had in store for him. And they would need many more strategies to help them take that work on.

By contrast, evaluation happens when readers take what they've come to understand about a text and consider its worth or merit, personally, intellectually, socially, or politically. As seen by their comments, the teachers in the workshop all found some value in the poem, yet not every reader finds worth in every text. Readers have a right to reject what they see as an author's message for all sorts of reasons—because it contradicts their own experience or because the author has failed to make a compelling case for how he sees the world. What is most important here is the act of considering and evaluating what a text and an author has to say, for it is in this process that reading becomes an act of self-definition, fostering insight and introspection, and advancing our awareness of who we are and who we might become.

We present these strands in this order because, generally, readers begin by comprehending and end with evaluation. But, as you no doubt have recognized as you've read beside us, the process isn't linear; it's actually recursive, with readers going back and forth between these modes of thinking as they draft and revise, connecting the dots and fitting the pieces of texts together. Additionally, the process doesn't ever quite end. We continue to make meaning as texts live within us, informing and coloring our lives, our choices, our opinions, even our actions. We hope, though, that by differentiating those words that are all too often used interchangeably in classrooms, we're enabling you to see how the pieces of reading fit together to create a rich, complex whole.

The Benefits of Being True to Our Own Experiences as Readers

USING TOOLS FOR AUTHENTIC PURPOSES

In addition to having created a new schema on which to attach professional learning—and hopefully feeling anew the satisfactions of deeply engaging with texts—connecting with ourselves as readers allows us to be better critical thinkers of the practices, structures, and supports often found in schools. We've seen how the way we can teach the main idea—as though it is something we can pluck out of texts, fully formed and there for the taking—runs counter to our own experience as readers and negates the critical role that details play in the process of meaning making. We've also seen that while we do use strategies such as connecting and inferring, we use them at particular points in the process for more precise ends than wholesale "comprehension." Similarly, while we use much of the academic language seen in our curricula and standards—as we did with the word *stanza* when talking about the poem—we always connect those terms to the process of meaning making. Thus, no teacher in the workshop simply identified the stanzas in "Food. Music. Memory." and left it at that; we all considered the stanzas only in light of how they contributed to our understanding. And no teacher talked about a personal connection with a hairbrush or a belt without coming back to the poem to consider what the poet might be saying through the use of those details. In effect, each reader was using literary elements and strategies as tools to make meaning, not as ends in and of themselves. Unfortunately, this is counter to what we see in many classrooms, where the teaching culminates in identification or isolated strategy practice.

When we have an authentic experience as readers, as we've had with Scavo's poem, we also find ourselves aware of the limits of some of the other language we use to talk to students about reading. Take what passes as conventional wisdom regarding the author's purpose: In many classrooms there are charts on the wall that identify the author's purpose as being one of three bullet points: to inform, to persuade, or to entertain. Yet how do those words correspond to Susan Marie Scavo and "Food. Music. Memory."? Was she trying to inform, persuade, or entertain us? And what about our purpose in reading? Was it the flipside to those chart bullet points: to be informed, persuaded, or entertained? Surely those words are inadequate to describe whatever compelled Scavo to write that poem and what we experienced through reading it. Yet we teach these purposes to our students and evaluate them on their ability to affix these terms to texts.

How much deeper—and truer to our own experience as readers—might our teaching be if, instead of using those words on those charts, we took our cues from our own reading lives and what writers have to say about their purposes? Here, for example, is the young adult writer Greg Neri (2009), talking about why he writes the books that he does, such as *Surf Mules*, the story of two high school students who make the disastrous decision to run drugs in order to maintain their surfer lifestyle:

> I'd like to think that my books can plant seeds in young people's head, so when they encounter situations in real life, they might have some knowledge to help them navigate . . . [A book is] one of the last mediums that truly allow you to think for yourself and interpret the actions going on before your eyes.

Neri wants his readers to actively think, not be passively entertained, informed, or persuaded. In particular, he wants the reader to consider the implications of his character's actions on their own life. One could say that he is trying to inform his reader, but not about surfing or drug trafficking—the facts about the content, which is what we usually mean when we talk about texts that inform. Rather he seems to want to inform us about the pressures and temptations that can push us toward bad choices, so that we might think and act with greater awareness and responsibility. In a sense, he is doing the very same thing Diane Ackerman said poets do: He is using the subject of drug-running surfers to explore a nugget of the human condition that intrigues, puzzles, or concerns him.

What would happen in classrooms if we taught students that this was the purpose of many, if not most, authors and that a reader's purpose was to contemplate those nuggets, both in texts and in their own lives? Throughout the rest of the book we'll share what this can look like in classrooms, but it is important to state here that it is only when we stay in close touch with ourselves as readers that we are able to plumb these depths. Our reading experiences need to serve as our rudder as we navigate through curricula and standards, data and assessments.

ASSESSING THE DEMANDS OF TEXTS

If we hold a steady course as readers who teach, we will not only be able to offer our students a deeper, more precise vision of reading and all the thinking it entails, we will also be able to assess and diagnose more precisely when, how, and why our students' meaning making occasionally or chronically breaks down. We acknowledged above that some of our ability to engage with a poem like "Food. Music. Memory." was related to the fact that it was within our comfort zone, neither too easy nor too hard a text for us to think about deeply. This is why it's so important to help students find those "just right" books—texts that are neither too easy nor too hard for them to access and engage with.

Summative assessments that gauge reading levels are useful tools for this, but pairing a student with the right level book doesn't guarantee that they'll read with depth. As leaders in the leveling field, Irene Fountas and Gay Su Pinnell (1996) have noted that leveled texts "offer the problem solving opportunities that build the reading process" (p. 113), but they do not, in and of themselves, ensure that students will avail themselves of those opportunities or solve whatever problems the text presents. Some students need a clearer vision of the work that readers do, and some of them struggle on the level of comprehension even in a book that is supposedly at their level. Additionally, if we look more carefully at books within any specific level, we can quickly see that while, in general, they may be "harder" than the level below them and "easier" than the level above, they are not always hard in the same ways, placing different demands on the reader.

Unfortunately, these demands are often not adequately or specifically addressed, even in materials provided by packaged leveling supports. Take for instance, the description of Level V provided by Scholastic's Guided Reading program:

Texts present complex issues and use technical language; topics are distant from students' experience in terms of time and geographic area, and may include realistic historical information and more difficult themes.

This description gives us a sense of the content challenges of Level V books, but it addresses none of the narrative and non-narrative challenges of such texts. Put another way, what's left invisible in this description is any mention of the complexity inherent in *how* they're written. If we are to instructionally support students in reading more complex texts, as the Common Core State Standards specifically ask us to, we must look more carefully at those challenges. Thus, to maximize our instructional effectiveness—and build ability through effort, not aptitude—we need to rely not only on those packaged assessments and other summative data but also on our own ability to assess both the demands of individual texts and how a student does or doesn't negotiate those specific demands.

In the following chapters we'll explore how we help students meet the different kinds of demands texts place on them (noting which chapters discuss which demands in our margin notes). But for now let's look more closely at what we mean by assessing the demands of the text by reading the opening of Patricia Reilly Giff's *Pictures of Hollis Woods*, a Level V text that we'll use again in Chapter 5. As we do so we'll think about how we know what we know and what we do with that knowledge as a way of making visible the work that readers do to both literally and inferentially comprehend this passage and begin to draft an understanding of the text's deeper meaning.

First Picture X

This picture has a dollop of peanut butter on one edge, a smear of grape jelly on the other, and an X across the whole thing. I cut it out of a magazine for homework when I was six years old. "Look for the words that begin with W," my teacher, Mrs. Evans, had said.

She was the one who marked in the X, spoiling my picture. She pointed. "This is a picture of a family, Hollis. A mother, M, a father, F, a brother, B, a sister, S. They're standing in front of their house, H. I don't see one W word here."

I opened my mouth to say: How about W for wish, or W for want, or W for "Wouldn't it be loverly" like the song the music teacher had taught us?

But Mrs. Evans was at the next table by that time, shushing me over her shoulder.

"Whoo-ee!" said the kid with dirty nails who sat next to me. "You don't know anything, Hollis Woods."

I reached for my crayon and dug an X into her picture of a snow-white washing machine. "Too bad you can't use it to get your hands clean," I said.

Let's take you through our own thinking now, which is probably an echo of your own. As we read this first page we came to know that the first-person narrator is named Hollis Woods. The author, however, hasn't told us that directly, the way she's told us that Mrs. Evans is the teacher; instead she's tucked the narrator's name into two lines of dialogue spoken by other characters, and we must infer that those characters are speaking to the narrator, which we do based on our understanding of how dialogue works and how narrative scenes often convey information indirectly. Similarly, we infer that the kid with the dirty nails is a girl because of the pronoun in the first line of the last paragraph: "I reached for my crayon and dug an X into her picture." We don't, however, know from these pages whether Hollis is a girl or a boy but we expect that we'll probably be given this information as we keep reading, perhaps directly or, as we think more likely, indirectly, since this text seems to be operating this way.

Figuring out what the characters are doing here is even trickier than comprehending who they are. On the one hand, we could say that Mrs. Evans is scolding Hollis for seemingly not doing a homework problem correctly. We say seemingly

Meeting the Demands of the Text: *We infer both the narrator's name and the gender of another character by drawing on our understanding that narrative writers convey information indirectly, tucking textual clues into dialogue and using pronouns in scenes. (see Chapter 3)*

because we had to infer from the line, "I opened my mouth to say: How about *W* for wish, or *W* for want, or *W* for 'Wouldn't it be loverly' . . . ,'" that Hollis did indeed consider the homework correctly done. We also infer from those same clues that Mrs. Evans and the dirty-nailed girl seem to think they are smarter than Hollis but that Hollis is probably smarter than either of them, and that Hollis wants, but doesn't have, the kind of family and house shown in the picture. From the fact that Hollis dug an X into the dirty-nailed girl's picture, we additionally infer that Hollis is angry, impulsive, and perhaps vindictive. These inferences, however, are slightly different than the ones we made to establish who the characters were because they are just hunches at this point; we know we will need to keep reading to gather more evidence and clues that will either confirm or challenge these first-impression inferences.

> **Meeting the Demands of the Text:** *From the details the author provides, we infer and begin to draft an understanding of what kind of person the narrator is, why she's doing, saying and feeling what she is, and how she sees the world, knowing that we'll develop and revise this understanding as we read on and learn more. (See Chapter 4)*

But something else is going on in this passage that complicates our sense of what the characters are doing. We know that this incident happened in the past both because of the line "I cut it out of a magazine for homework when I was six years old" and the following verb construction, "my teacher, Mrs. Evans, *had* said." From these small details and textual clues, we infer what is actually happening here: Hollis is looking at or thinking about this picture and recounting its history from some point after the incident happened. But nothing in this passage gives us any clues about when and where that present moment is. We expect that this might be made clear as we keep reading, as we also expect that we will get some clarity about why this passage is written in italics. And so we know we have to postpone clarity at the same time that we expect clarity—not just about what is going to happen but about all of the choices the writer has made. Complex texts tend to require readers to postpone clarity for longer periods of time and about more aspects than simpler texts.

> **Meeting the Demands of the Text:** *By attending to textual time clues and verb tenses, we infer that this incident took place in the past and is being recollected by the narrator in some still-to-be-determined present moment. (See Chapter 3)*

> **Meeting the Demands of the Text:** *Expecting clarity as we read on, we hold on to the questions the text has raised– why is this passage written in italics; is Hollis a boy or a girl; when, where, and why is this being recollected–knowing that we may find clues to the answers if we read on attentively. (See Chapters 3-5)*

Combining all these inferences with our awareness that authors often plant the seeds of a book's larger issues in the opening scene, we immediately begin to develop a hunch about a possible main problem in the book. We think it may revolve around Hollis' desire for a family and a house. And if our initial inference is right about Hollis not having a family and home, we also wonder if the reason he or she doesn't is connected in some way—be it cause or effect—to the portrait we are beginning to develop of an impulsive and maybe vindictive person. And we wonder if, in the quest for a home, Hollis will find someone who is more sympathetic than Mrs. Evans and the dirty-nailed girl—as we begin to realize that we are already rooting for this person as we turn the page.

Meeting the Demands of the Text: *Connecting the inferences we've made so far, we begin to develop a hunch about the problems Hollis is facing; and in wondering about how those problems might be solved, we invest ourselves emotionally in the character and the story in a way that helps us get our first glimmer of the possible themes of the book. (See Chapters 4-7)*

We can see here how many demands this passage places on readers—and how many problems they must solve, at the sentence and paragraph level—just to literally and inferentially comprehend. These demands are very different from other Level V texts, where readers may have to juggle shifts in time or points of view with only the subtlest of textual clues or keep track of a barrage of details whose significance becomes apparent only much further in the text. They may also be different than the demands of whatever passage was used to assess students at this level. Thus there is no guarantee that every student assessed at a given level will meet the specific demands of each text at that level without specific strategies for dealing with these demands. And while it might be tempting to see these demands as inherent to high-level texts, there are many texts from Level K on up that present similar challenges, from following dialogue to inferring about characters and synthesizing each part to think about the whole. Without more precise instruction—about how texts work and how a mind works within texts—many readers have little chance of ever accessing and engaging with the themes and issues that lie beneath the literal layers of texts, let alone contemplate how those issues and themes might impact their own lives.

But before you run to your classroom and start delivering minilessons on pronouns and how to follow dialogue, we urge you to hold your horses. Remember, this book is not just about what to teach but also how, and we believe that the two are essentially entwined. As we try to demonstrate in the following chapters, students need to know about concrete challenges that texts place on readers but they also need to experience, in authentic and meaningful ways, what that knowledge allows them to do.

Chapter Three

How Readers Draft and Revise Their Way from Confusion to Clarity

Perplexity is the beginning of knowledge.

—Kahlil Gibran

We are in a fifth-grade classroom, walking around the room conferring with students, when we see a student just starting a book, *From the Mixed-Up Files of Mrs. Basil E. Frankweiler* by E. L. Konigsburg (1967). The teacher we're working with steers us away. "Taraya is just beginning that book. Let's wait and confer with her next week," he suggests, "when there's something to talk about." We're familiar with this impulse—that reading conferences have to be about the content of books, which students can only begin to discuss once they're further along. But as we saw when we looked carefully at the opening of *Pictures of Hollis Woods*, beginnings place many demands on readers and are often complicated. And so we decide to go ahead and confer with Taraya right now.

We approach her just as she's finishing the letter that opens the book, prologue-style, and turns the page to start Chapter 1. As we ask her about what she's thinking, she demonstrates that she already knows something about this book: She points to the cover photograph to tell us about the character, Claudia, and her brother, Jamie, and how they run away to the Metropolitan Museum of

Art. When we ask how she knows this information, she turns the book over and points to the blurb.

"I see you just read this page," we say, opening the book again to the prologue to return to the actual text. "What were you thinking when you read that?" Though we've read the book before, we quickly scan the page. It's a letter that opens "To my lawyer, Saxonberg" and is signed "Mrs. Basil E. Frankweiler." It contains no references to Claudia or Jamie or a museum or art.

Taraya sits in silence for a bit, and as she does, we reflect on what we should teach. Should we teach her what a prologue is and why it's important? Should we teach her to think about titles as she reads, since this letter has the words *file* and *Mrs. Basil E. Frankweiler* in it? Should we teach her to make predictions based on information that's in the letter? But as we ponder, we also wonder what her silence means. As teachers, we often interpret silence as meaning "I don't know" and rush to fill it with our knowledge. We have been challenging ourselves not to do this, not to always put our students on the receiving end of that knowledge but to consider, via Peter Johnston, what thinking they may be doing that we could notice and name. In this case "I don't know" could be a response rather than an indication of a deficit. How else can a reader take in the opening section of this book, which seems to have nothing to do with the characters and the situation that this student has read about in the blurb. We decide to notice and name for Taraya the accuracy of her silence and the power inherent in it.

"Your silence tells me that you may not know what to think about this letter," we begin. "And you know what? I think that's a really accurate response! It is really confusing. We have no idea what this letter or the characters mentioned here have to do with the rest of the book. But I don't think we're supposed to know. I think the author probably wants her readers to go, 'Huh?' just like you did. She can't expect us to know who these characters are or what they're talking about or what this has to do with the story that's about to start. But she probably doesn't want you to just shrug and forget about it either. Sometimes authors plant confusion, and if readers hold onto questions they have, they'll get answers eventually. I bet that by the end of the book you'll have some clue about what this letter might mean and maybe even why the author chose to open the book this way."

When we return to this class the following week, Taraya comes bolting up to us, holding her book open with excitement. "Here it is!" she says, and when we look puzzled she goes on: "The answer to the beginning. It says it here," and she reads the following sentence from page 123: *And that, Saxonberg, is how I enter the story. Claudia and Jamie Kincaid came to see me about Angel.* "Mrs. Franken-whoever is telling the story!"

How impressed we are that this ten-year-old has held her confusion all the way through the book, through all the twists and turns of the story, over the course of a week of reading, until at last it begins to make some sense to her. How confident we are that as she continues to read on from page 123 to the end, her understanding of the opening letter as well as why the author chose to use it in that way will deepen, and with it her understanding of the many layers of this book. How powerful, we realize, are the words "We don't know—yet."

What We Do as Readers

WE KNOW THAT CONFUSION IS A NATURAL RESPONSE TO HOW NARRATIVES ARE WRITTEN

We knew to say this to Taraya because this is exactly what we experience ourselves as we read. Her silence and the question mark it seemed to contain are indicative of the confusion readers often experience when they plunge into a text. Who are these characters? What's going on here? When and where is this taking place? Why is the author telling me this? What could it possibly mean? There is so much to figure out and so much we don't know that's it natural to feel a bit overwhelmed and even downright lost. In fact, confusion is almost an inevitable by-product of the way narratives work. With both *Pictures of Hollis Woods* and *The Mixed-Up Files of Mrs. Basil E. Frankweiler*—as well as many other texts at lower levels—we are far from the forthright narrative technique found in fairy tales, where an omniscient storyteller provides us with some context and an introduction to the character, before leading us with the words "One day" into the action of the story. In the case of *Hollis Woods*, for instance, that kind of straightforward opening might sound something like this: "Once upon a time there was a girl named Hollis Woods who never had a family of her own. She wanted one desperately, but no one understood that—not her teacher, nor the girl in her class who told her she was stupid. But then one day . . ." Instead, author Patricia Reilly Giff plunks us down in a scene in which she slips information in sideways, tucking the narrator's name into a line of dialogue, giving us details through which we must infer something about her life, while not in any way making the time frame or the setting clear, nor providing us with any background information that might explain why Hollis was so desirous of a family and a home.

This method of presenting a narrative through dramatized scenes is one of the many ways writers practice the writing workshop mantra of "show, not tell." They convey information indirectly via details that act as textual clues. And nowhere is this more challenging to readers than right at the beginning of a text. We can feel lost and disoriented as we start to read, as if we've been teleported to a party already in full swing, where we must scramble to catch up, sorting out quickly who's who and what's what, if we have any chance of joining in. In addition to factual details about the who, what, and where of the story, we're also often given a slew of other details that we have no idea what to make of. Some are there to bring the scene to life, to render it fully and vividly so that we can see and feel it. Others, as we'll explore in Chapter 4, are conveying information about what kind of people the characters are, why they are doing what they're doing, and how they relate to each other. Still others have been purposely planted early on and will play a part in whatever drama the writer has in store for her characters, and some of these will be repeated, as we'll see in Chapter 5, to create what we might call a recurring motif in the book's overall design. These, as we'll explain in Chapter 6, can be used to help construct an understanding of a book's theme.

The problem is that, as first-time readers with no idea of where the book is headed beyond, perhaps, the blurb, we don't know which detail is which. We can only be sure that they've been chosen deliberately for some purpose, and so we must try to hold onto them until that purpose becomes clearer to us, which is not always easy. Fortunately, however, experienced readers know how to deal with these challenges. They bring their understanding of how texts work with them whenever they read. And they have a few strategies up their sleeves, which we explore below.

WE DRAFT AND REVISE OUR WAY OUT OF CONFUSION, KNOWING THAT WE'LL EVENTUALLY FIND CLARITY

One thing that helps readers tolerate the confusion that beginnings frequently engender is the knowledge that much of what initially puzzles them will eventually become clearer. Readers know this because they understand how texts are put together, with writers not only writing in scenes that show instead of tell, but planting details whose significance will become more apparent as the story unfolds. This was, in fact, what Taraya learned when she reached page 123 and finally was able to understand that odd and confusing beginning. What she needed to do, though, was begin drafting her take on the text right away, noting that at page one what she understood so far was that there was a character named Mrs. Basil E. Frankweiler who was writing to her lawyer about some files that she seemed to have written. Then she had to keep reading on, looking for more clues that might help her revise and develop that draft, trusting that everything would add up and make sense—eventually.

In this way, she was doing exactly what we did when we slowed down our thinking to examine how we made sense of the poem "Food. Music. Memory." We saw there that when we read the first words—*She says*—we simultaneously took in the words as providing information we knew (a pronoun, a female, someone talking to someone else) as well as pointing toward information we didn't yet know (who is this "she" and who is she talking to?). We held onto those questions, expecting to get clarity as we continued reading. And so when we read the words *I say* at the beginning of the second stanza, we thought, "Ah, this must be the 'I' who 'she' is talking to," and we revised our sense of the text accordingly. And with that, new questions came into our heads—such as, what is "she's" relationship with "I," and what are they talking about?—and we read on once again, expecting to uncover more that would help us answer those questions and enable us not just to comprehend, but to ultimately understand and interpret.

Proficient readers tend to draft automatically, often with such speed we hardly notice. But making the process visible for less experienced readers allows them to both see and experience how readers connect and accumulate text from sentence to sentence, page to page, and chapter to chapter across a whole book. And it helps those students monitor their comprehension more actively as they read, because they are reading forward looking for clues that will help clear up their natural confusion and add to their understanding.

WE INFER TO ESTABLISH A CONTEXT FOR THE SCENES THE WRITER PROVIDES

With book-length narratives, our initial drafts are usually attempts at creating a context for the scenes the author gives us. We read closely, looking for those textual clues that might let us know who the characters are, what seems to be happening, and when and where they are, in order to get a foothold on the story and orient ourselves. To do so, we often have to make what Donna Santman in *Shades of Meaning* (2005) calls a "figure it out" inference—one that yields factual information that's ultimately not open to interpretation as other inferences are (though we sometimes need to read further on before we are absolutely sure). We made many "figure it out" inferences, for example, when we assessed the demands of *Pictures of Hollis Woods* in the previous chapter. We inferred the name of the narrator from a name in a line of dialogue, the gender of the kid with dirty nails from a pronoun, and the fact that the event with the X'd out homework picture happened sometime in the past from a verb construction (see page 49).

In other texts, we might have to infer the location of a scene or a shift in time from a tiny detail or figure out an event or something that's happened from a handful of details that show, not explicitly tell—and all of this can be tricky. In fact, not every reader manages to catch every textual clue, but knowing that writers plant clues in this way encourages us to look out for them and to read more attentively in general. And the good news is that authors often give us several chances to figure things out, giving us additional clues in case we missed the first ones. What's needed, though, is an alert and receptive mind, along with some basic understanding of the way texts work, revealing and clarifying information over time, often in indirect ways.

WE EMBRACE NOT KNOWING, UNDERSTANDING THAT IT SERVES A VITAL PURPOSE

Finally, our ability to tolerate confusion and be comfortable with postponing clarity is connected to our sense that not knowing is actually very useful. If we knew everything right from the start, there would be no point in reading on. Not knowing is what propels us forward; it's what keeps us reading, turning the pages of a book, or reading and rereading a poem. It keeps us engaged and, perhaps more importantly, it keeps us invested in the text, allowing us to experience the story, much as the characters do themselves, as we move from confusion to clarity, overcoming obstacles and gaining knowledge and insight as we go.

What we know, though, as readers that we sometimes forget as teachers is that this "not knowing" is very different from not comprehending, though the two are often confused—and both can cause confusion. To clarify this, let's go back to "Food. Music. Memory." again. In the first stanza we would not be comprehending if we failed to recognize that there were two characters, the "she" who says, "I was there," and a "you," she's speaking to. No matter how much we'd comprehended, though, we wouldn't know who the "you" was at that point, and no number of fix-up strategies would help us, because the author hasn't yet revealed that (though the line *All I taught you* combined with other details might lead some readers to draft an understanding that the "you" could be "she's" child). In any event, we'd keep on reading expecting to find out more and to clarify some of what we had initially found confusing.

This idea, which fluent readers seem to know instinctively, seems to baffle many children. Perhaps our teaching is partially to blame: Perhaps we habitually refer to confusion as a problem that needs a "fix-up" strategy rather than stopping to consider, as we did with Taraya, that confusion is not always the same as lack of comprehension. Perhaps we would better serve our students if, instead of rushing to fill silences with answers, we helped them become aware that answers reveal themselves as we read, that they grow out of a process of drafting and revising that, in turn, is born from attending to details. Perhaps we'd do better if we celebrated confusion—both our own and theirs—as the place from which understanding and real learning begin, as John Dewey noted way back in 1910 in *How We Think*, or as Nancy Willard has written more recently in her book *Telling Time* (1993), "Answers are closed rooms; and questions are open doors that invite us in" (p. 129).

And so, in this chapter's lesson, we aim to make the following visible to students:

* Meaning making is a process requiring constant drafting and revising.

* Confusion is a natural part of this process because narratives are constructed from scenes that "show" instead of "tell."

* Readers deal with this confusion by holding onto details to create a context for the scenes the author gives them and prepare for what may come next.

* Readers tolerate confusion but expect clarity—eventually.

What This Sounds Like in Classrooms

We sit in the back of a classroom in Brooklyn, facing a rug filled with curious third graders, a book on our lap and chart paper on an easel beside us. The book is *How to Steal a Dog* by Barbara O'Connor (2007), a story about a girl named Georgina who must deal with the unintended and complicated consequences

What we do as teachers: *We choose a text that supports our enduring understandings as well as our immediate teaching goals.*

of her decision to steal a dog in order to help her family out of a financial jam. We've chosen the book for two reasons: It's a perfect example of how a text can invite us to think about our lives and the actions we take in the world; and it is written in a way that will help us demonstrate our main teaching points—that readers draft and revise their way from confusion into eventual clarity by attending to the details authors provide.

Of course, we don't quite say this to the students. In all classes we are aware of the need to balance talk and practice, and with eight- and nine-year-olds, in particular, too much talk about how-to or why is likely to be counterpro-

What we do as teachers: *We use the structure of read-aloud to introduce students to the thinking work of reading.*

ductive. We want our teaching to come from what the students are doing and experiencing in a text and so have decided to jump into the read-aloud relatively quickly, with a minimum of talk. We settle everyone down and introduce the book in the following way:

"Today we're going to start a new book together: *How to Steal a Dog* by Barbara O'Connor." We show the cover, which has a simple photograph of a dog reaching for a dog biscuit that's dangling from a string, with the words *A NOVEL* stamped on it.

"When readers first start books," we tell the students, "we know nothing, really. OK, maybe you read the blurb on the back cover or a friend or your teacher may have read it and told you something about it, but pretty much when a reader first starts reading we don't know who the story is about or what's going to happen or why. We read in order to find out all that stuff. That's the fun of the story. So at the beginning of a book it's natural that a reader sometimes feels lost—like they've been plopped down inside a character's head and don't have a clue about what's going on. That's the way this book works. It plops us right into the middle of a story, without giving us a whole lot of background. So to help us as we read, we're going to keep track of our thinking, jotting down

What we do as teachers: *We provide students with a tool to help them produce their own meaning.*

what we're discovering and paying attention to the clues that help us know that and also jotting down what we're wondering and expect to find out as we keep reading."

We draw a line down the middle of the chart paper to create a two-column graphic organizer. We write WHAT

WE KNOW as the heading on the left column and WHAT WE WONDER as the heading on the right (Figure 3–1).

What We Know	What We Wonder

Figure 3–1. A two-column KNOW/WONDER chart to help students keep track of their thinking

Then we read the first sentence: *The day I decided to steal a dog was the same day my best friend, Luanne Godfrey, found out I lived in a car.*

What we do as teachers: *We begin to read without engaging the students in any prereading activities.*

We reread the sentence and turn to the chart, modeling how to use it.

"So what I know from the first sentence is that there's a character who decided to steal a dog because it says 'The day I decided to steal a dog.'"

We write *Character decided to steal a dog* under the KNOW column of the chart.

A few students raise their hands, seemingly ready to add on to our thinking, and we invite them to do so.

"What do you know from this sentence?" we ask a boy.

"He lives in a car," he states definitively.

This is immediately interesting to us because of the student's use of the word "he." Nothing in this sentence has, in fact, revealed the character to be male or female, and though the pronoun "he" is often used generically—and that is probably how this student intends it—we decide to use this comment to push into the WHAT WE WONDER side of the chart.

What we do as teachers: *We seize opportunities to use student thinking to demonstrate our lessons rather than always using our own.*

"Yes," we respond, "there *is* something about living in a car here." We reread the sentence again so everyone can follow. "So we know that this character lives in a car." We write that down on the chart. "But," we continue, "you also said something else interesting—you said '*He* lives in a car.' How do you know it's a 'he' who lives in the car?"

"Oh," the student flushed, his confidence brought down a notch. Of course we didn't mean to embarrass him or make him feel judged, so we jump in to reassure him.

"'Oh' is such a great thinking word, so thank you for that. You helped us realize that we *don't* know something. We actually *don't* know whether this character is a boy or a girl, do we?" We explain that often what readers don't know is what we wonder about and expect to be answered—somehow, at some point in the story—as we read on.

"That's the kind of thing we can put under the WONDER side of our chart." We add "Is the character a boy or a girl?" to the WONDER column.

Our initial modeling of the two columns complete, we prepare to continue reading when another boy raises his hand.

"It could be a dog," he says seriously.

"What do you mean?" we ask.

"The character," the boy responds, "it could be a dog. Like a boy or a girl or a dog."

We take a breath. On the one hand this feels like a comment that might distract us from our purpose. We look at the WONDER column, afraid that perhaps it is too open-ended. Perhaps we need to seize control and steer this student back to what we know—that this is realistic fiction and dogs don't narrate these kinds of books. But, we remind ourselves, we are here to teach the thinking around the text, not the text itself, and so we decide to explore the origins of the student's comment.

What we do as teachers:
We don't evaluate students' responses but rather always ask, "What made you think that?"

"Tell us," we ask, "what part of what I read made you think the character could be a dog?"

The boy stands up solemnly, tiptoes over the students sitting on the carpet in front of him, takes the book out of our hands, and shows everyone the cover.

Of course. The cover shows a photograph of a dog. Why couldn't the character be a dog? We think of other books with main characters who are animals acting in human ways, books this student may very well be reading. Rather than saying something silly or distracting he is actually bringing his knowledge of texts—his schema—to his reading of this text, which is something we certainly want student readers to be more aware of.

"So based on the cover," we say, "you think this could be the kind of book, perhaps like *Frog and Toad* or *Poppleton*, where the main characters are animals who talk."

The student nods, and we write "Is the character a dog?" under the WONDER heading on the chart and continue to elicit students' wonderings.

"Why did he steal a dog?" asks one.

"Why does he live in a car?" asks another.

We write these questions down, and move on to the next few sentences of the book. We reread the first sentence again—*The day I decided to steal a dog was the same day my best friend, Luanne Godfrey, found out I lived in a car*—and then keep reading. *I had told Mama she would find out sooner or later, seeing as how she's so nosy and all. But Mama had rolled her eyes and said, "Just get on up there to the bus stop, Georgina, and quit your whining."*

Several students' hands shoot up as we finish the paragraph.

"What are you thinking? What do you know or what are you wondering?" we ask.

"We found out the character's name," says the first student we call on.

"How did we find that out?"

"It says so. The mom says it — 'Georgina,'" the student responds.

We call on another student waving her hand eagerly.

"And she's a girl!" this student exclaims. "We got an answer to that—" she points to the question in the WONDER column. "Is the character a boy or a girl?"

"What makes you think it's a girl?" we ask.

"Georgina. It sounds like a girl's name."

"It could be a boy," interjects another student.

This is a prime example of what happens when texts "show" rather than "tell" information: Readers will understand them in different ways and at different points along the story. One person's KNOW column won't necessarily match that of another. We decide this may be a good opportunity to highlight this and the drafting and revising work these students have done so far.

"Let's pause here and talk about the thinking we've done together. Right now a few of you are pretty sure that the narrator's name is Georgina and that she's a girl. A few of you are still wondering if it could be a boy or maybe a dog. Because the writer doesn't come right out and tell us these things, we have all been getting our information from clues the writer is giving through the story.

The author has given us a few clues, but not that many, so we're going to keep reading and try to pick up on more clues that the author might provide. We

What we do as teachers: *We trust the process of drafting and revising to take care of possible, and natural, missteps.*

might get more solid clues that confirm what some of you already think—that the narrator is a girl—or we might get some clues that the narrator is, in fact, a boy or a dog, and we'll have to revise our thoughts based on those clues."

To show students how, even within a few sentences, some of us have moved from wondering something to knowing something, we take a pencil and lightly draw an arrow from the question in the WONDER column, "Is this character a boy or a girl?," to the KNOW column and write "The character is a girl." The pencil, however, is to acknowledge that some of us need to keep reading in order to continue picking up on clues that will either confirm what we know or require us to revise what we think we know (Figure 3–2).

What We Know	What We Wonder
Character decided to steal a dog	Why?
Character lives in a car	Why?
	What is the character's name?
Georgina	
	Is the character a boy or a girl?
The character is a girl	
	Is the character a dog?

Figure 3–2. The KNOW/WONDER chart with students' thinking from the first few sentences of *How to Steal a Dog*, with a penciled-in arrow indicating a possible answer

We look out at the class, reminding ourselves about the balance between talk and practice. It's probably time to continue reading. We know we will have many opportunities to return to and reinforce this teaching as we move through *How to Steal a Dog* and begin working with small groups and individual students as they read other books. We also plan on giving students opportunities to do some of the KNOW/WONDER work orally, with partners, rather than exclusively as a whole class, and to make their own KNOW/WONDER charts in their reading notebooks. But for now, for these students, it's time to delve into the rest of the chapter uninterrupted.

What We Do as Teachers

Sometimes reading lessons feel like nesting dolls: We peel the top off of one teaching point only to reveal another, smaller one tucked inside, which in turn contains an even smaller one, which opens to yet another one. The lesson we did with this third-grade class certainly fits in this category. Reading is complicated work and one lesson can't possibly be about just one aspect of that thinking. Yet we owe it to our students to be clear, explicit, and focused. In this section we will unpack our teaching, taking the lid off some of the explicit points we made with these students as well as some of the implicit points we made. In addition, we will look more closely here at our methodology—how we taught the lesson—that helped support the content we were trying to convey.

WE TRUST THE PROCESS OF DRAFTING AND REVISING TO TAKE CARE OF POSSIBLE, AND NATURAL, MISSTEPS

From examining our own reading, we recognize that faulty steps are a natural part of thinking in a text and want our first lessons to name this as children experience it for themselves. In particular, we want them to know the difference between not knowing yet, which is a natural by-product of how texts reveal themselves, and not comprehending. We do this first by explicitly stating that this is the way most narrative texts work and then demonstrating how readers navigate these texts as we plunge together into the first pages. Our trust in this process allows us to be comfortable with the fact that not every student's comprehension will look exactly the same at exactly the same time. While a consensus will most likely emerge about what is literally happening in the text, we do not aim for this in any one book—and certainly know that when it comes time to interpret and evaluate, we will see, and celebrate, the many and varied ideas that stem from one text. But even early in a book, when readers are trying to ground themselves in the who and the what of a story, we think it far more important for each student to see and experience how specific words help them know what they know than for the class to reach perfect agreement about what we know from a text.

This, then, is the focus of our teaching—allowing meaning making, and the roots of that meaning, to be visible for each student, whether that work is initially just figuring out the name or sex of the character or whether it is something meatier, such as pondering why a character is doing a certain thing. We therefore are not likely to stop in the middle of our reading and comprehend *for* students, whether explicitly, by jumping into a discussion to prove one student right over another, or implicitly, by stopping at key points in a text and asking our own comprehension questions of the students.

Rethinking our practice: *We don't stop to ask comprehension questions as we read aloud.*

WE TRUST OUR UNDERSTANDING OF HOW TEXTS WORK TO EVENTUALLY CLARIFY NATURAL MISSTEPS

Just as we trust the process of drafting and revising, we also trust the text to eventually clarify possible missteps in comprehension. We know that stories work by often "showing" and not "telling"—whether it is something simple such as the name of a character, or something more complex such as a theme. We also know that, because information is revealed through the story, most texts don't provide one clue and one clue only about issues requiring either literal or inferential comprehension. Rather, they layer information, touching on a point, then touching on it again and perhaps again. For example, about whether Georgina is a girl or a boy, we are given a piece of information—a name—which some students interpreted or know to be a female name. But to the child who said "It could be a boy," we can trust that the text will clarify this point over time, probably and most immediately in the form of a pronoun, but maybe also in a more direct way such as the brother saying something like, "I hate my sister." Texts work this way, and if we teach students the power of reading attentively, we trust that they will pick up on textual clues that will eventually clarify their comprehension.

WE DON'T EVALUATE STUDENTS' RESPONSES BUT RATHER ALWAYS ASK, "WHAT MADE YOU THINK THAT?"

Because we trust the process of reading and the way texts work, we don't tell a student if their thinking is right or wrong but rather ask them where they got their thinking. We also don't correct or censor what we put on the KNOW/

WONDER chart during these initial lessons and try not to insert our own understanding of a text into our teaching. Our goal, after all, is to teach the process of making meaning, not to direct the students to a particular meaning.

So, for example, when we modeled the use of the KNOW/WONDER chart from the first sentence in *How to Steal a Dog*, we wrote the word "character" instead of "she," because our knowledge that the "I" is a girl comes from our prior reading of the book. Furthermore, when we read on and a student said that the narrator's name was Georgina, we could have said, "Yes!" because we made the same inference. Instead, we asked her to explain how she concluded that and acknowledged, by using pencil on the class chart, that this might not be an inference everyone made from the same clue. We hope, of course, that other students will notice and consider the textual clues that enabled this reader to make this inference—in this case the reference to her name in a line of dialogue—but will save our explicit teaching of that strategy for a small-group or one-on-one conference.

WE PROVIDE STUDENTS WITH A TOOL TO HELP THEM PRODUCE THEIR OWN MEANING

We have chosen the KNOW/WONDER chart as the main tool we use in beginning-of-the-book lessons because it is simple and open-ended and allows students to see the invisible process of their reading: how attending to details helps readers forge through confusion to draft and revise meaning. The chart allows us to capture the powerful thinking inherent in words such as "maybe" and "I think" that readers use when they first start reading and words such as "ohhhh" and "aha" as they read on toward clarity. The chart also allows us to turn much of the demonstration work of our lessons over to the students' thinking rather than our own. With these third graders, we initially demonstrated how to use the chart, but after that all the content of what went onto the chart came from the students.

But as much as we have designed this chart for the use of our students, it helps us as well, by keeping us focused on our task as facilitators of thinking. Without the WONDER column in front of us as we read *How to Steal a Dog*, for example, we may easily have been swept into a discussion about the specifics of the text—whether the character was a dog or a girl, or what her name was.

Rethinking our practice:
We focus our teaching on the students' thinking in a text rather than dwelling on their specific thoughts.

The thinking chart reminds us that our ultimate task is to remain teachers of thinking, not conveyers of thoughts.

WE CHOOSE TEXTS TO SUPPORT BOTH OUR LOFTIEST ENDURING UNDERSTANDING AND OUR IMMEDIATE TEACHING GOALS

We choose books for our initial read-alouds that first and foremost demonstrate why we read—in Alfred Tatum's words (2009), books that "provide guidance and road maps for being, doing, thinking and acting" (p. 23). We then link to that end whatever strategies our students might need—based on what we know about them, about the process of reading, and about the text—in order to teach them how to read. To help us do this job, we tend to gravitate toward books that are character driven, by which we mean a narrative, whether it's fiction or nonfiction, whose plot is determined as much by the character's personality, actions, and choices as by external factors. We also look for books that are accessible enough for students to grasp the big picture of reading without struggling too much with literal comprehension. We don't want a text with an overly complicated structure or plot or challenging vocabulary or one that requires a huge stretch in terms of background knowledge. We do, however, look for books that have enough twists and turns that students will have to revise their thinking as a matter of course, and we look for books that have multiple entry points and implications so that students can see that meaning making is, ultimately, a complex and personal journey between a reader and a book.

Rethinking our practice:
We choose texts to support the value of reading and the process of making meaning rather than to practice strategies.

WE USE THE STRUCTURE OF READ-ALOUD TO INTRODUCE STUDENTS TO THE THINKING WORK OF READING

Over the years we have seen read-alouds used in a variety of ways: to focus students at the beginning of the day; to transition a class from recess back to work mode; as a reward or send-off at the end of the day; to build community by exploring issues at play in students' lives; to let off steam and get giggles out. In a sense, all these uses are a testament to how powerful a read-aloud can be, and many a teacher has described their read-aloud time as the best part of their day.

Students seem to agree, applauding the announcement that brings them to the rug, moaning with disappointment when there isn't time for one more chapter, and letting out a sigh of satisfaction when the teacher says, "The End."

On the one hand, we don't want to tamper with something that offers both students and teachers alike such a positive experience, but the very fact that read-aloud is so compelling and enjoyable makes it the ideal platform from which to offer students an introduction to the big work of reading. We can explicitly provide them with an opportunity to experience all the components of meaning making, especially those parts, like the work of inferring, under- standing, and evaluating, that often remain invisible, in a supportive social setting. Being exposed to such a vision of reading also gives children something concrete to transfer to their independent reading, and it offers us a common language and foundation to refer to when we talk with students in conferences and small groups.

> **Rethinking our practice:** *We use read-aloud to introduce the foundational thinking work of reading, not just to build community and engagement.*

WE BEGIN TO READ WITHOUT ENGAGING THE STUDENTS IN ANY PREREADING ACTIVITIES

For many teachers, the fact that we tend not to engage in any prereading activities such as reading the back blurb, predicting from the cover, or accessing background knowledge, is startling. Studying covers is an incredibly useful strategy to employ when choosing something to read, and we always encourage students to do so when they're in the market for a book. In most cases where we are doing read-aloud work, however, we have chosen the text, which makes the use of the strategy for that purpose moot. Likewise, we would have read students the blurb if we'd been practicing test-taking strategies, when we would specifically teach them to support their comprehension by using every available resource a text selection offers, including introductions, directions, illustrations, and captions.

When we read *How to Steal a Dog*, however, we refrained from reading the blurb because it would have undermined one of the main purposes of our initial lesson, which was to heighten the students' awareness of one of the ways writers show rather than tell information and how readers have to draft and revise their comprehension based on textual clues. We wanted the students to do that thinking in a way that would allow them to make their own meaning from the very first page. Additionally, hearing the blurb would have deprived them of the excitement of figuring information out for themselves, and it wouldn't have fostered the kind of attention and alertness readers need when tackling beginnings. We saw this clearly when we spoke with Taraya who, relying on the blurb of *From the Mixed-Up Files of Mrs. Basil E. Frankweiler* to steer her through the first pages, seemed ready to glaze over the prologue.

Similarly, we didn't ask the students to predict what the book might be about from the cover. Once again, looking at covers is useful when selecting a book to read, and it can be a helpful strategy for certain nonfiction texts whose visuals have been purposefully chosen to position readers around a central idea, but inviting students to predict based only on the title and the cover can open the door to unsupported speculation. Experience has also shown us that students can become wedded to an initial prediction, ignoring all kinds of textual clues that don't conform to their idea. In effect, predicting from the cover narrows students' thinking down to one idea at the precise moment when they need to be the most open and flexible. It is simply premature to predict before we have any sense of where the author might be taking us. Additionally, it is time consuming, and the goal of getting readers to be actively engaged can be better met by opening the book and jumping into the words on the first page.

Rethinking our practice: *We question the purposes behind standard practices, such as prereading activities, rather than doing them as a matter of course.*

Making Every Student's Thinking Visible

HELPING STUDENTS INFER FROM SUBTLE CLUES USING A "STEPPED-UP" APPROACH

While the above lesson gives every student a feel for how readers draft and revise their thinking in order to literally and inferentially comprehend and orient themselves at the beginning of a text, we're all too aware that classrooms are diverse. No matter what grade you find yourself teaching, you'll inevitably have students in your class who have different experiences with texts and read on different levels. In that third-grade class, for instance, most children were not yet reading at the level of *How to Steal a Dog*. While our fluent reading of the text out loud allows each student to comprehend words they may have trouble decoding independently, we're aware that not every student will pick up on many of the subtler textual clues that allow a reader to inferentially comprehend. Even as we trust the process of drafting and revising to straighten and flush out miscomprehensions, we believe it is our job to help every student meet the challenges of increasingly complex texts. What is often most complex about these texts is what is most invisible, i.e., places that require a reader to infer. We therefore need to build ability through effort by designing instruction that specifically builds a bridge between what is visible in texts and what is invisible.

One way we do this is through what we call a "stepped-up" lesson that's aimed at helping a small group of students be more aware of what they already know how to do in a text that's at their level in order to do the same work in a more complex text. In this example, we are teaching students about textual clues that provide information about time, place, situation, and character that readers use to visualize, comprehend, and orient themselves in the beginning of texts. In this approach, we begin with a text in which we think each of these students will be able to notice the textual clues that give them this information, and then plan on incrementally stepping them up into texts where these clues are subtler or indirect. Our role as teachers in this small group is to notice and name the work they're doing in a way that builds their agency and ability.

We share here a set of "stepped-up" texts that we've used with small groups of third and fourth graders to help them better see the subtle clues authors provide about where a scene is taking place (Figure 3–3). As we can see if we attend to the demands of each text, none of the authors directly state where the character is, which means that in order to visualize and follow the scene, a reader must make an inference from clues the author provides. In *Nate the Great* (2002) and *Amber Brown Sees Red* (1997), we infer where the characters are from what the authors show us they're doing. The clues around this are more visible in *Nate the Great* since the narrator comes right out and says what he is doing, whereas the narrator in *Amber Brown* states what she's doing in a slightly less direct way. In *Judy Moody Was in a Mood* (2000), the author creates an additional challenge by telling us what the character is *not* doing in a way that reveals where she is.

Nate the Great By Marjorie Weinman Sharmat	*Amber Brown Sees Red* By Paula Danziger	*Judy Moody Was in a Mood* By Megan McDonald
My name is Nate the Great. I am a detective. I work alone. Let me tell you about my last case: I had just eaten breakfast. It was a good breakfast.	I, Amber Brown, am going through a growth spurt. Either that or the mirror's getting smaller. I keep looking at myself from different angles. Either my eyesight is getting bad or my bangs are covering my eyes. I can practically feel myself getting taller . . . My new shoes that I got only two months ago at the beginning of fourth grade are too small. I'm not sure that I'm ready for this growth spurt.	Judy Moody did not want to give up summer. She did not feel like brushing her hair every day. She did not feel like memorizing spelling words. And she did not want to sit next to Frank Pearl, who ate paste, in class. Judy Moody was in a mood. Not a good mood. A bad mood. A mad-face mood. Even the smell of her new Grouchy pencils could not get her out of bed.

Figure 3–3. Text-set example for "stepped-up" lesson on inferring where a character is

When we meet with students for any lesson, we begin by framing the work we'll be doing around the larger work of reading—telling students what this lesson has to do with what readers do and the way texts operate. In this case we state that texts operate by plopping readers right into a scene, so it's important that readers orient themselves in the beginning of books. We do this by paying attention to clues that tell us who the characters are and where they are. We share with these students why it's important to do this work, telling them that knowing where the characters are helps us picture the story, which in turn helps us follow the story and feel like we're there side-by-side with the characters.

We then read the first text, *Nate the Great*, aloud to the students, providing them with copies so they can follow along. When we reach the end of the passage we ask students where they think Nate is. Typically we get several answers to that question—e.g., "in his house," "at a table," "in the kitchen"—and when we ask what led them to think that, most children point to the accompanying picture, which shows Nate sitting at a table with a plate full of food in front of him. When asked if, in addition to the picture, there are any words or sentences that suggest where Nate might be, many children, with time and encouragement to read the passage again, point to the line, *I had just eaten breakfast.* From there we notice and name the thinking work they did to figure out where the character was—they noticed a picture and a sentence that described what the character was doing. We then offer this as a strategy to use with the next text, *Amber Brown*, which we give to the students without the picture that appears in the book to better help them practice the strategy with only the words of the text.

Most students have no clear idea of where Amber is in this scene; their eyes glide over the clues in the second and third sentences that tell us that she's standing in front of a mirror—in her bedroom or, perhaps, a store dressing room; that much we don't know yet—and allow us to quickly conceive a picture of a girl scrutinizing her reflection in a mirror and pondering the changes of her body. In the past, we might have directed the children to those sentences, prompting them to look at the words that gave us meaning with a question such as, "What do you think Amber Brown is doing *here*?" But we now believe that doing so would make the students dependent on us and deprive them of the agency they need to construct meaning. So instead we remind them of the strategy that enabled them to know where Nate was in *Nate the Great*: "You knew where Nate was because you knew what he was doing. Knowing that authors do that, you can reread this section for clues that tell you what Amber Brown might be doing and see if that can give you a clue about where she might be." When reminded that they already know how to do this, the students immediately point to the sentence that gives them direct information about what Amber Brown is doing: *I keep looking at myself from different angles.* They then conclude that she's looking at herself in a mirror, which may be in her bedroom or house.

We then say to the students that in this text the clues are subtler than they are in *Nate the Great*. "In this text the reader is plopped down inside Amber's thoughts. The writer doesn't come right out and say what she's doing, the way the author of *Nate the Great* did. You had to read a little more carefully, purposefully asking yourself what the character was doing. But you now have an idea—that she's looking in the mirror and may be in her bedroom or house."

We urge the students to hold onto this idea as a draft, reading on to see if the text will provide additional clues that will confirm that idea or require them to revise. We then read on with them, turning the page and coming to the following sentence: *Sitting down on my bed, I picked up my favorite stuffed toy.* As we read that sentence each student interrupts with an "Oh," or "Ah." "What?" we ask. "She's in her house," they say, or "She's in her room." "How do you know?" we ask, and they all point to the sentence that provides information about what she's doing, sitting on a bed.

Again we notice and name their thinking, repeating the strategy that enabled them to visualize where the character was in this more difficult text: paying attention to clues that gave information about what the character was doing. We also noticed and named the process they employed that allowed them to do this successfully: drafting an understanding that was then confirmed as they kept reading. Our next steps depend on our students and on how much time we have: We could either proceed in a similar manner with the third "stepped-up" text or save it for another session.

WHAT THIS LESSON ALLOWS STUDENTS TO DO

What this lesson allows students to do is to become more aware of what they already know how to do so they can practice it in more deliberate and meaningful ways. In this case, we have highlighted a strategy that they have used that can help them do the work of two big skills: visualizing and inferring. This strategy allows them to "see," as it were, how textual clues operate in texts, which allows them to move from something that is right there on the page to something that is subtler. In addition, the lesson allows students to experience how readers hold onto drafts of understanding and read on to confirm or revise those drafts. This will become increasingly important as they read texts that reveal information in direct as well as indirect ways. They have to read closely, attending to details in a way that helps them accumulate meaning as they read and lessens the likelihood that they will become lost and in need of a fix-up strategy later on.

Finally, the lesson demystifies the process of arriving at an "aha" moment in a text; this is no longer the domain of the "capable" readers in the class. Each of these readers has constructed his or her insight from clues *they* have picked up, and each of them can "see" and experience what this insight looks and feels like. This is a "can-do" moment for them, which increases their engagement, and also provides agency that they can carry into other, progressively complex texts.

For all these reasons, we love the stepped-up approach and have used it at every grade level for all sorts of comprehension challenges in texts, including:

* Navigating shifts in time

* Figuring out who's saying what to whom in dialogue

* Following pronouns

* Drafting an initial impression of a character through the details the author provides

* Inferentially comprehending imagery

* Following syntactically complex sentences.

All you need to do to plan a stepped-up lesson is the willingness to open a book and think about yourself as a reader. What do you know about what's happening on a page in a book and how do you know it? It's the question we also need to ask our students as we confer with them. For in answering that question we begin to make visible the invisible work of making meaning in ways that allow us to design instruction that empowers each student as a reader.

Rethinking How We Teach Reading	
What We Used to Do . . .	**What We Do Now . . .**
We used to pause in read-alouds to ask the students comprehension questions.	We orchestrate and facilitate experiences for students that allow them to pose and answer their own comprehension questions.
We used to evaluate student responses in various overt and subtle ways (e.g., by saying "You're right," or "Let's think about that more" if a student's response seemed off-the-mark).	We trust the process of reading to weed out unsupportable thinking or missteps, asking students instead, "What made you think that?"
We used to model our teaching point through our own thinking.	We draw on student thinking to model teaching points whenever we possibly can.
We used to select read-aloud texts in order to teach particular reading strategies (e.g., we'd look for a text that was good to teach visualization or predicting) or to build community and engagement.	We choose texts that invite students to experience both the deeper, most enduring reasons for reading and the drafting and revising process of meaning making.
We used to ask the students to do certain prereading activities (e.g., predict what the book was about based on the cover, read the back blurb, do a picture walk) as a matter of course.	We think about how those prereading activities do or don't serve our larger purposes and often refrain from doing them in order to show students how to elicit information from the actual words in the text.

Making It Work: Some Practical Tips for Implementation

Making Sure Our Tools Serve Our Larger Purposes

Our KNOW/WONDER chart is an incredibly useful tool for making the process of meaning making visible, but as with any strategy or scaffold we give our students, we want be careful that our means don't become our end. Here, for instance, we want to ensure that our desire to make the thinking work of reading visible through the use of a chart doesn't overly interfere with the need to provide students with the rich, engaging reading experience that will produce and inspire that thinking. Put another way, we want to always make sure we are charting to read, not reading to chart. And to that end, we do the following:

▶ We **slow the process down in the very beginning** to give students a chance to actually experience the work that readers do–in this case how readers revise their understanding of a text as they pick up the textual clues that will help clarify their confusion. Once the class has experienced that firsthand, we read for longer stretches of time so students can become more immersed in the story without so many interruptions.

▶ Over time, **we chart less and have students talk more**, doing the work we initially made visible through the chart orally, rather than in writing, and adding to the chart only when a student has made an insightful comment, said something we could use in a future lesson (as you'll see us do in Chapters 4, 5, and 6), or when we want to boost a student's confidence by honoring their thinking.

▶ We **ask students to keep their own charts** in their reading notebooks, either for homework or at the end of the period, and give them the opportunity to share out before or after the read-aloud.

▶ We **chart more in the beginning of the year**, when we're first introducing this thinking, than we do as the school year goes on and students are more familiar with the work we have been noticing and naming with them. We return to the scaffold of the chart, however, when applying and transferring the thinking to different genres or to more difficult texts.

Chapter Four

How Readers Infer
the Significance of Details

Caress the detail, the divine detail.

—Vladimir Nabokov

We are in a classroom working with a small group of fifth-grade students who we know need additional practice on navigating beginnings. To support them, we've chosen a text, *Just Juice* by Karen Hesse (1999), that is actually below their assessed independent reading level but presents many challenges of the sort we described in the last chapter. We remind the students of what we've been working on, picking up small textual clues that help us figure out the who, what, when, and where of an opening scene. And we reiterate why this is so important—because writers don't always come out and introduce us to the characters or their situation in a direct way; instead they plop us down in a scene where we have to figure out what's going on in order to get an initial grasp of the story and not be so confused.

Then we give them the following passage from the first page of Chapter 1, which is titled "Brown Paper Bags":

> "Where's Juice?" Ma says, spreading grape jelly so thin on the sliced
> white bread, you can hardly find the purple. "If she doesn't get herself

to school this morning, that truant officer'll be here before I can finish breakfast dishes."

"Won't matter when he comes, Ma," Charleen says. "He won't find Juice, and even if he does, he can't make her stay in school. He'd have to tie her to Miss Hamble's desk to do that."

I hide outside on the back porch, watching them through the window. My fingers rest on the rough wood. Markey, my older sister, looks out at me. But she doesn't make one peep about where I mought be found.

As we suspected, the passage is not so easy for the students, especially when it comes to recognizing that Juice is the "she" who seems averse to school, not a drink as they all first thought, and that this "she" is also the "I" who is narrating the story. To comprehend this, they had to first recognize their confusion, then talk to each other and go back to the text, looking hard for those clues the author has planted that ultimately allow them to infer the who, what, when, and where of the scene.

Doing this fills them with the sense of accomplishment that effort-based instruction can bring. They're thrilled, just as we are, with how they've been able to draft and revise their way out of confusion by attending to those textual clues. And we're sure this experience will encourage them to read more attentively when they return to their independent reading. Yet as we read the passage alongside them, we're struck by something in the very first sentence. We notice the detail about Ma spreading jelly, "so thin on the sliced white bread, you can hardly find the purple," and we wonder if that detail is not only "showing" us that Ma is in the kitchen, but "telling" us that the family is poor, or perhaps that Ma is thoughtful or indulgent, customizing a sandwich for a child who likes her jelly light.

Either way, as proficient readers, we are sure it means something beyond just establishing a location for a scene. And that suspicion is confirmed as the students continue on to the next page and we notice another detail about the brown paper bags of the chapter's title that the mother packs her children's lunch in: "Even after I've used the bag all week and it's limber as a dishrag, I still like opening it and taking out that jelly sandwich" (p. 2). Aha, we think, here's another detail that seems to be suggesting poverty, though like the jelly, the students glance over it in part because they're unaware that details such as these carry meaning.

On the one hand, just like textual clues, we assume that, if this information is important, the writer will return to it as the text unfolds, providing readers with more opportunities to catch that the family is poor. On the other hand, we want to raise students' awareness that writers choose details purposely and that we, as readers, can burrow deeper into the text if we consider what those details might be "telling" in addition to "showing" us. And so we pause to consider what to do. Should we draw the students' attention back to the paper bags and the jelly, prompting them with leading questions that all but tell them what to think? Should we try to seize this as a teaching moment, offering some impromptu on-the-spot instruction about inferring other kinds of information beyond the who, what, when, and where?

Having done the former ourselves before, we know that it risks demoralizing our students and leaving them feeling defeated precisely when some of them are feeling empowered as readers for the first time. And it lands us right back in that unwanted role of the gatekeepers of meaning. As for the latter, while it might be doable, it also runs the risk of undermining the success the students are feeling by putting something else on their plate that they may not be quite ready for. And so we remember the reading equivalent of the writing workshop tenets to teach the writer, not the writing, and keep our lessons focused. With that in mind, we decide to let those details go and save that teaching for another day, when we can design a more in-depth lesson, of the kind we present below, that helps students see how readers infer to access not just contextual information but deeper levels of meaning from the details the author provides.

What We Do as Readers

WE READ WITH AN AWARENESS THAT DETAILS CARRY MEANING

As readers we know that details are the building blocks of texts. They are divine, as Nabokov says, in the sense that they're the raw material or matter from which writers create resonant stories, constructing scenes, establishing characters, even developing themes. As we saw in our lesson in the previous chapter and the small-group work above, we use certain details to gather basic information, frequently via inferring, that narrative writers don't deliver directly but instead weave into scenes. And we hold onto others, whether we immediately grasp their importance or not, because we know that they might reappear and play some role as the story unfolds, just as the letter that mysteriously opened *The Mixed-Up Files of Mrs. Basil E. Frankweiler* did—123 pages later.

But we also know something else about details: They are frequently more than they appear, carrying significance or meaning beyond the literal. As writer Flannery O'Connor (1969) once wrote, these kinds of details are ones "that, while having their essential place in the literal level of the story, operate in depth as well as on the surface, increasing the story in every direction" (p. 71). We saw this clearly in "Food. Music. Memory." where the details referred to literal, concrete objects—a hairbrush, cupcakes, Kahlua—while also conveying "significant" information about each of the characters, their relationship to each other, their history together, and ultimately, when taken all together, the theme. In this instance, we could also say that these details "signified" abstract ideas— for many the hairbrush signified abuse, the cupcakes conveyed nurturing or care, while the thin spreading of jelly and the reused paper bags in *Just Juice* suggested poverty. They showed *and* told simultaneously, though unlike the textual clues we explored in the previous chapter that revealed definitive, factual information, what these details "tell" can be open to various interpretations, as we saw with the jelly, and they often require us to keep reading to confirm or revise our thinking.

This concept that details in texts reveal significant information about characters, their feelings, motivations, and problems, along with their relation- ship to others is often challenging for children to grasp, though, in fact, they and we do it all the time in life. We notice someone tapping their foot and conclude that they're annoyed or impatient; we categorize people by the clothes they wear, seeing the labels and styles they choose as indicative of who they are or who they want to be. And we often realize that there's a subtext beneath the words we say to each other, with our speech often revealing how we relate and feel about each other in addition to whatever information we're directly conveying. In each of these instances we "read" something into a small detail that we notice, and while what it suggests may not tell the whole story about any given person or relationship, it does allow us to form a first impression, which we, too, revise and reconsider as we continue to learn more.

When it comes to classrooms, this understanding about the role of details is implicit in the prompts we give to our students and the essay topics we assign, and it underlies many of the questions found in standardized tests and teacher guides. Yet, like "show, don't tell," it is something we discuss and explicitly teach more in writing than in reading. When faced with a narrative written by a student, for instance, that dutifully recalls all the events of a particular day—often from the moment they wake up to the moment they go back to bed—we ask them, "Why was this important to you?" We ask because we know that events recounted without underlying meaning are ultimately unsatisfying to read. And we hope, by asking, to help draw out whatever significance might be buried in the piece so that the child can go back and revise, using that deeper meaning as a guide to decide what parts to leave in and highlight and what parts to leave out, choosing specific details more deliberately to bring that meaning out.

In this way we ask our student writers to deliberately choose details that not only show but tell and to arrange and fit those details together so that the underlying meaning is more apparent, just as real writers do. Too often, though, we don't ask students to read with this same corresponding understanding in a way that would actively engage them in considering what meaning the writer hoped to convey through his choice of detail. Thus we often see students reading as if the text were a bed-to-bed story, a series of sequential events that may be exciting, funny, or sad, but that haven't been purposely orchestrated by the author to reveal some deeper meaning, with specific details carefully chosen to develop and support that. And unless we make this more visible to students, we cannot expect them to take on this work in an active, deliberate way.

WE ACCESS THE SIGNIFICANCE OF DETAILS BY INFERRING

When we "read" annoyance in the tapping of a foot or poverty in a thin smear of jelly, we are, in fact, inferring, though how we infer and what these inferences sound like is different than the way we inferred in the last chapter. There we helped students pick up textual clues that allowed them to infer factual information that was conveyed indirectly in order to create a context and make sense of a scene. Here, we can say that inferring is the tool that helps us move from the specific to the more abstract—from a hairbrush to abuse, from Kahlua to alcoholism, and from a thin smear of jelly on a slice of white bread and reused paper bags to poverty. Put another way, the inferring we explored in Chapter 3 allows students to comprehend the text, while these inferences move us from comprehension into the realm of understanding, where deeper meaning resides.

As opposed to "figure-it-out" inferences, Donna Santman calls these "making-more" ones, and what's also different between these inferences are the strategies we use to infer. In the last chapter we drew on our knowledge of how pronouns, dialogue, and scenes operate in order to infer who, when, and where the characters were, and what was going on. Here, we draw on our understanding of how narratives are most frequently structured around characters who have one or more problems, which writers frequently introduce early on through those indirect details that both show *and* tell the why's and the how's of the text: Why are the characters acting they way they are and how are they feeling about that? What kinds of people do they seem to be and how is that helping or impeding them from dealing with whatever problems the author has put in their way?

Because we know this is how narratives are structured, when we open a narrative, as we did with *Just Juice*, our reading antennas are already up and on the lookout for details that might help us understand what kinds of problems the characters are facing and how they might be dealing with them. And so, when we encountered the detail about the jelly, we automatically asked ourselves, why would a character be doing that? What might this detail mean? In particular, what might it be telling us about the nature of the character or the situation they're in?

To consider those questions, we drew on our understanding of people and life. In this sense, you could say we made connections, but our understanding about the way narratives are structured helped us filter out whatever random connections we might have about jelly sandwiches and focus only on those that suggested ways in which this detail might reveal something about the character or their problems. In this way our connections were highly purposeful and directly tied to our understanding of how narratives operate. Put another way, you could say that we had a strategy for the complicated skill of inferring: to draw on our own experience and knowledge to specifically consider what a detail might be "telling" us about a character or a potential problem.

We then brought our inference back to the text and added it to the understanding we were in the process of drafting. But we didn't lock in on it uncategorically, as if our inference was the single right answer. Instead we kept our minds open and read on, knowing that within the world of the text, this detail might signify something different than it does in our own life and world—just as the hairbrush in "Food. Music. Memory." meant something different in the world of the poem than hairbrushes did in many readers' lives. We also knew that whatever it meant would become clearer as we read on and encountered other details that would either confirm or challenge our initial first-draft suspicion. In this way, making-more inferences are similar to predictions or hunches, a term we'll explore more below. And the whole process of drafting and revising our understanding of these details is a bit like the scientific method. We observe phenomena, which in reading means noticing the details the author is providing, and from that we posit a hypothesis through inferring about the significance of those details. Then we test out our hypothesis as we keep reading, attentively noticing subsequent details that either support our hypothesis or compel us to revise, until we feel we've gathered enough evidence to turn our hypothesis into a theory, which in reading we call an interpretation.

WE KNOW THAT TEXTS PROVIDE MULTIPLE OPPORTUNITIES TO ACCESS AND CONSTRUCT MEANING

While the process of understanding begins with a heightened awareness of how narratives are structured and how writers use details to tell, not just to show, we don't as readers—or as teachers—need to catch the significance of every detail. This is because we know that texts provide us with multiple opportunities to construct meaning and that different readers will pick up on different details depending on who they are, what they notice, and what they bring to the text. While our *Just Juice* readers, for instance, didn't catch the paper bags or the jelly, many did notice the strange word *mought* at the end of our reproduced passage. And while, at the level of comprehension, they inferred that *mought* meant "might," they also wondered why Juice would say that, asking themselves what it might mean that she used that particular word instead of the more common *might*. Others, meanwhile, continued to read forward to learn why Juice didn't want to go school. All of these students picked up on the fact, which the author conveyed directly, that she had been left back, and one student noticed a subtler detail that she didn't quite know what to do with that actually provides a further clue to Juice's trouble at school: that Juice "pretend-reads" to her younger sisters.

Any of these details—the jelly, the paper bags, the word *mought*, and the pretend-reading—are, in effect, entryways to the deeper meaning of the text. None is inherently more important than the other, and no one inference about them is necessarily "right"—especially at this point in the text when the story is just starting to unfold. What's important is not which detail readers notice, but what they do with them—that is, how they infer a first-draft hunch of what those details might be telling based on their knowledge of how texts work and the other details they encounter. And so, in the lesson that follows we attempt to show students what they can make with what they notice. We do this by designing and orchestrating an experience that helps them infer the significance of a detail, then to use that inference as a tool to dig deeper and begin to consider the why's and the how's that lie underneath the events. Additionally, we aim to make visible the following understandings about readers and texts that we draw on as we read:

* Details often carry significance that, if considered, will lead us deeper

* Texts operate at multiple levels, exploring the why and the how, not just the what

* Readers begin to consider these hidden levels by thinking about what individual details might be "telling" us

* Readers infer by knowing how narratives are structured and connecting details within the text.

What This Sounds Like in Classrooms

We are in a middle school in Manhattan's Hell's Kitchen where we are reading *Miracle's Boys* by Jacqueline Woodson (2000) to a class of seventh graders. The book tells the story of three half African American/half Puerto Rican brothers living in New York City who must learn how to cope and survive as a family after their mother dies. The oldest brother, Ty'ree, has dropped out of college to take care of his siblings; the middle brother, Charlie, has recently returned from a juvenile detention center where he was sent for reasons that, at this point in the book, haven't been revealed. He's come back so changed, though, that the younger brother, Lafayette—a seventh grader, like our students, who's also the book's narrator—has taken to calling him Newcharlie as a way to differentiate him from the person he loved and knew.

As we did in our third-grade example, we've chosen the text because it is one of those books that can act as a road map for living and also because accessing that road map requires the exact kind of process of reading we want to make visible to students. Also like our third grade exercise, we began the read-aloud with an acknowledgment that beginnings are confusing. And we used the same KNOW/WONDER chart as a tool to help the students hold onto what they were learning and what they were wondering about, as well as to "see" and experience firsthand how readers revise their initial thinking as the story unfolds. (See Figure 4–1.)

What We Know	What We Wonder
The narrator has a brother named Newcharlie & another brother, Ty'ree.	Who's talking and who are they talking to?
Newcharlie's talking to Aaron.	
	What's the narrator's name?
The narrator's name is Lafayette.	
Newcharlie's been away at the Rahway Home for Boys.	Why did he go there?
Newcharlie's real name is Charlie but the narrator calls him that because he seems like a different person since he came back from Rahway.	Why did he change? Will he change back again?
The old Charlie had lots of feelings about things, especially for stray animals.	Does he still care about animals?
Their mother died.	How did she die? Why?
Newcharlie's hated Lafayette ever since their mother died.	What does "Later, Milagro killer" mean? What did Lafayette mean by "I didn't kill her"?

Figure 4–1. The KNOW/WONDER chart from the first chapter of *Miracle's Boys* with arrows indicating questions that were answered as students kept reading

This day we return to the chart to dig deeper into the text. We use one of the students' wonderings to make visible for the class what can happen when we follow Vladimir Nabokov's injunction to "caress" a detail by connecting it to others in order to consider its possible significance regarding the deeper layers in the book. Like our previous lesson, however, we try to express this in kid-friendly language, beginning by first reminding students of the work they've already done and reiterating for them how what they've done as readers is connected to the way texts work. We then connect that to this day's focus as follows:

> **What we do as teachers:**
> *We build the lesson from the students' thinking, not our own.*

"We've been talking about how authors don't always come right out and tell us everything we need to know right up front, even basic things like who's talking to whom and where the characters are. Instead they slip information in, planting clues they expect us to catch, just like we expect them to reveal more over time and make certain things clearer as we read. Spotting those clues the other day we were able to figure out who the narrator was, who was talking to whom and where they were. We also got a beginning sense of what was going on. But we still had lots and lots of questions about what some particular lines meant and why characters were saying and feeling the things they were, which are really great questions to ask because authors frequently explore why people do the things they do and how they cope with their problems.

"But once again, writers don't often come out and tell us directly. Instead they give us little details that are a bit like puzzle pieces or the dots in those connect-the-dots games you see in puzzle books. They show us a little part of the answer, and it's our job as readers to try to connect the details the author is giving us and fit them together so we can see—or begin to get a glimmer of—something that she might be trying to tell us about both the characters in this book and people and life in general.

"So today I want to go back to one of the details that caught your attention and made us wonder, the line where Lafayette says, 'I didn't kill her,' to see if this might be a piece of the puzzle that ultimately might give us some ideas about the why questions we had. That line came right at the end of the chapter, which is a place where authors sometimes spring surprises on us or purposely leave us hanging so that we want to keep

> **What we do as teachers:**
> *We build the lesson around our assessment of the demands of the text.*

reading—which is exactly what happened to us. We were really, really curious about what that meant and why he said that. So let's see if that line might be connected to anything we've already figured out or know that's on our chart in a way that might give us some new ideas about both what that line might mean and some of our other why questions."

What we do as teachers:
We provide students with a customized strategy and protocol for inferring.

To help the students stick to the text, we project a copy of the chapter's last page on the screen for everyone to see (Figure 4–2) and position the KNOW/WONDER chart nearby. We also ask the students to work with a partner, suggesting that, if nothing leaps to their mind, they go down the KNOW side of the chart item by item, considering if anything might be connected to our wondering. We also remind them that there's no right or wrong; it's just the thinking that matters. Then we hunker down with a couple of partners as the students turn and talk, reconvening the group after a few minutes so the students can share out.

> *"You ready?" Newcharlie asked.*
> *Aaron nodded.*
> *"Then step up." He looked at me. "When Ty'ree gets home, you tell him we just left too, you hear me?"*
> *I kept staring out the window.*
> *"Your brother talking to you, man," Aaron said.*
> *"Yeah—I hear you."*
> *"Later, Milagro killer."*
> *"Oh shoot." Aaron laughed. "That's cold, man."*
> *"It's true," Charlie said.*
> *I swallowed and looked down at my hands so Newcharlie wouldn't see my eyes tearing up. . . . It was gray out. I stared at the sky and tried not to let his words sink in. I stared until the window blurred.*
> *"I didn't kill her," I whispered.*
> *Then I lay back on my bed and prayed it would pour down rain.*

Figure 4–2. Passage from *Miracle's Boys* (pp. 14-15) used in the lesson

"Okay," we begin, "so what are we thinking?"

Some hands go up, a few of them waving almost frantically, and we let one of those eager students start us off.

"Maybe Lafayette means he didn't kill their mother."

"Wow," we say, "what made you think that?"

"Well, we connected the question to what we know. And we know that Mama died."

"Yeah," says the student's partner, "and Mama's a 'she' and Lafayette says, 'her,' 'I didn't kill *her*.'"

"Great thinking," we say. "That's certainly possible—especially since you really showed us how the idea came from the text." Then, as we did with the third graders when some students inferred the name and gender of the narrator in *How to Steal a Dog*, we use pencil to circle the word *mother* on the KNOW side of the chart and draw a line to connect it to the word *her* in the sentence "*I didn't kill her*" that appears in our WONDER column. This indicates that, while a student's made a good connection, we may need more clues before every student in the class is sure that this is what Lafayette means.

At this point, several more hands shoot up.

"And that could be why Newcharlie hates Lafayette, because he killed their mother," says one student as others nod their heads.

"Yeah, and maybe Newcharlie got blamed for it and that was why he was sent away to Rahway."

Once again, as we did with our third graders, we pause for a moment. From our own prior reading of the text, we know that neither of these is true, and we feel that little tug of worry that, amid all these spiraling speculations, the students may be starting to wander into the land of unsupported conjecture. But we recognize that at this point in the text, these ideas are, indeed, possible, and we trust that the process of drafting and revising combined with close, attentive reading will help the students ultimately weed out the ones that can't be supported by the text. So instead of stepping in to "correct" or rein in their thinking, we decided to honor it and name for them what they're doing: developing hunches about the bigger ideas that lurk below the surface in texts.

What we do as teachers: *We choose the language we use to teach strategies to best capture the work readers do.*

"You guys are really on a roll here! First of all, I love the way all of you are saying 'maybe' or 'could be,' because we don't really know the answer for sure yet. But by connecting some of these details, we have a lot of really interesting ideas that are sort of like hunches. We think we might have some answers, but we're not absolutely positive yet. That's exactly what happens as we start to put parts of the story together, connecting the details like puzzle pieces or dots. We begin to have hunches about what's going on underneath the surface of the book—what we could call the story under the story—based on all these clues the author is giving us.

"As we keep on reading, I'm sure we'll learn more, but I'm wondering now if anyone else noticed other details that they think could be connected to both our original question about what Lafayette meant when he said, 'I didn't kill her,' and to these two new ideas or hunches about why Newcharlie hates Lafayette and why he might have been sent to Rahway."

We let the question sit in the air for a moment, giving the students a chance to look back over both the passage and the chart. Then a student raises her hand.

"Newcharlie calls Lafayette a 'Milagro killer.'"

"Hmm," we say. "That's really interesting. Can you say more about that?"

"Well," the student says slowly, "I'm thinking that when Lafayette says, 'I didn't kill her,' he's responding to Newcharlie calling him a 'Milagro killer.' So what he means is he didn't kill 'Milagro,' but Newcharlie thinks he did."

"That's pretty amazing thinking, as well. We wondered what a Milagro killer was yesterday, and now you're connecting it to what Lafayette says. Even if we're not absolutely sure yet who or what a 'Milagro' is, we think that Newcharlie is calling Lafayette a killer of Milagro, and we're pretty sure Lafayette's saying that he didn't kill Milagro. We also thought Lafayette might have meant their mother since she's a she and we know that she died. So . . . it's possible that Milagro refers to their mother," we say as we once again pick up our pencil and draw arrows between our wonderings and what we know about the mother.

Then one of our Spanish-speaking students raises his hand. "Or Milagro could have something to do with the title, because 'milagro' means miracle and the book's called *Miracle's Boys.*"

"Oh my! Not only are you all connecting what we wondered about with what we know, but now you're connecting it with the title—all from looking and thinking about one little detail in the book! That's incredible. So let's stop here for a moment, and write down some of the hunches we have about what might be going on between these characters and why they may be saying, doing, and feeling what they are. Because it's so early on in the book, I'm going to put them down as questions on the wondering side of our chart" (Figure 4–3).

What We Wonder
▶ Does Newcharlie hate Lafayette because he killed their mother?
▶ Does Newcharlie just think Lafayette killed their mother, even though he didn't?
▶ Was Newcharlie sent to Rahway because he was blamed for killing their mother when it was really Lafayette?
▶ Does "Milagro" have something to do with the title (because of the word *miracle*)?
▶ Is "Milagro" their mother?

Figure 4–3. New wonderings generated by connecting details and inferring

We wrap up the lesson by reminding the students to be on the lookout for other details and clues that might add additional support to any of these hunches or make us reconsider and revise, because, as we've seen, thinking about details can unlock the hidden depths of a story. Then we open the book and the students lean forward, with a deeper, stronger sense of engagement palpable in the air.

What We Do as Teachers

WE BUILD THE LESSON FROM THE STUDENTS' THINKING, NOT OUR OWN

As we saw in our previous lesson, the KNOW/WONDER chart supports students in a variety of ways. It helps them keep track of their thinking, see the process of drafting and revision in action, accumulate text from page to page, and read more attentively in a way that allows those deeper "why" questions to emerge naturally. It also helps us maintain our stance as teachers who facilitate thinking, not those who, in overt and subtle ways, sanction specific meaning. Here it offers additional benefits. While we began our seventh-grade read-aloud just as we did the third-grade one, with a brief demonstration of what we meant by keeping track of what we're learning as we read, the chart allows us to begin this lesson with the students' own thinking, not ours. This is significant for several reasons.

As Peter Johnston so wisely notes, "When children notice things, instruction can begin with a joint focus of attention because the children are already attending" (p. 18). Here, because the students had already noticed the detail we used to support this day's lesson, they were more invested and receptive to considering what its significance could be than they would have been if we'd had to draw their attention to it.

Additionally, Johnston cites studies that have shown that young children whose mothers follow their lead, practicing what researchers call "attentional following," have stronger vocabularies than children whose mothers try to get them to focus on something they, not the child, deem important, which requires "attentional shifting" by the child. We cannot claim to have increased the students' vocabulary here, but we do believe that the energy and engagement the students exhibited, both during the lesson and in the subsequent read-aloud, is directly linked to our "attentional following" of the students' lead and the increased confidence they felt in their ability to read with more depth and insight than many had experienced before.

Finally, when students truly own the meaning they're making of a text—when they're the ones accumulating details and seeing how the pieces all fit—they're far more likely to monitor their comprehension because it is actually *theirs*. And while every reader sometimes needs to go back and pick up a detail they missed, like a knitter picking up a slipped stitch, slipped stitches are far less likely when students are reading with the kind of attention and engagement that comes with a sense of ownership.

WE BUILD THE LESSON AROUND OUR ASSESSMENT OF THE DEMANDS OF THE TEXT

While we try to build lessons around student thinking whenever we possibly can, our instructional decisions are also informed by what we recognize as the demands of the actual text we're using and how, as readers, we meet those demands. In this case, as readers, we sensed the significance of the two details the students had noticed—when Newcharlie calls Lafayette a Milagro killer and when Lafayette says, "I didn't kill her"—both because of their strategic placement at the end of the chapter and because we were already actively hunting for clues that might help us understand why the brothers' relationship seemed so strained. As readers, we also knew that we had to infer to both comprehend what *Milagro killer* meant on the literal level—i.e., that Newcharlie was accusing Lafayette of having killed their mother—and to consider what this detail might be telling us about the kind of person Newcharlie is and the brothers' relationship, along with how they were dealing with the problems they faced in the wake of their mother's death. We did that, just as the students did, by connecting these lines with other details we had noticed, though for us that thinking happened so quickly it almost seemed automatic. And like the students, the inference we made yielded many questions about the why's and the how's of the text, and those questions, in turn, became the basis of what we might call a line of inquiry that we would follow and actively explore as we continued to read, just as the students did.

All of this made these details ideal as a starting place for a lesson that aimed to help students see how writers plant details that operate on more than one level and how readers develop hunches around their inferences to begin to explore the text's *whys* and *hows*. And so we do direct students to one of the details they've noticed, based on what we recognize as readers will most support our goals. In this way, the students provided the entry point, but we provided the tools.

WE PROVIDE STUDENTS WITH A CUSTOMIZED STRATEGY AND PROTOCOL FOR INFERRING

With the *what* of our lesson in place, we still must consider the *how*—as in how are we going to help students see the particular work that readers do with these kinds of significant details. Some experts suggest always beginning by helping students access their prior knowledge or providing them with background information, which in the case of *Miracle's Boys* might mean eliciting or frontloading the meaning of the word *milagro* or discussing the setting of Spanish Harlem. Others recommend using think-alouds, where the teacher walks the students through the various strategies and thought processes she used to make meaning of a text, as a way to make explicit and visible the work that readers do.

We certainly have done both of these in the past, though increasingly each feels problematic. When it comes to supplying background information, we do believe that there are times when it can enhance and enrich a student's reading experience—for example, with certain nonfiction texts, which assume that the reader will have some familiarity with the topic in general. But when we frontload information about the content or context of a narrative text, we run the risk of reinforcing the idea that students cannot deeply engage with a text unless they already have some knowledge about its content. We also deprive them of the critical-thinking and problem-solving opportunities that narrative texts provide.

Narratives provide these opportunities because, in effect, they are self-contained worlds constructed, from the inside out, of interwoven details that give us virtually all we need to know in order to understand them—provided we know how to read them. We seem to know this instinctively when we enter the realm of science fiction or fantasy, where it never occurs to us to frontload, say, information about the social hierarchy of Muggles and Truebloods before reading Harry Potter. There we know that the text will create its own context and world for us, which we can access provided we read carefully and stick close to the text, connecting detail to detail and page to page as we draft and revise our way toward meaning. Yet we seem to forget this when it comes to realistic and historical fiction, rushing in once again to provide outside information

Rethinking our practice:
We give students a chance to construct an understanding from the details of a text rather than automatically providing background information.

rather than letting the students see what they can make with what the author gives them, often by inferring the significance of details. In the case of *Miracle's Boys*, for instance, what the word *milagro* means outside of the text is far less important than what it means in the context of the text—and the only way we can understand that is by engaging in the thinking work of reading, not by accessing background knowledge.

With think-alouds, similar problems exist. Their ostensible purpose is to show students *how*, not *what*, to think, by modeling how readers use strategies to make meaning. Yet frequently we've found that what students take away is *what* we made of the text. So while we could have done a think-aloud here, demonstrating for the students how we connect details in order to infer what they might be "telling" us beyond the literal surface, in the end we'd be producing a reading of the text, rather than giving the students the tools for producing a reading of their own, which is precisely what Robert Scholes warned us against doing, as we saw in Chapter 2. And so rather than modeling through a think-aloud, we reframe what we invisibly do as an explicit strategy—we connect what we wonder to what we know from the text in a way that allows us to consider what a detail might be "telling" us—and we offer it to the class with a step-by-step protocol—going methodically down the list of what we know to consider any possible connections—for the students that need it. This method allows the students to actively experience, rather than just passively watch, the exact same thinking process we once would have modeled through a think-aloud, while leaving the product of that thinking work—the insight and the hunches the students arrived at—theirs and theirs alone.

Rethinking our practice: *We offer students tools for constructing their own meaning, rather than always using think-alouds to model ours.*

Additionally, we believe that this type of strategy is more effective than the kind of one-size-fits-all strategies for inferring we often see in schools, such as, "It Says, I Know, and So," which asks readers to connect what the text says with what they know from their own lives in order to infer what a particular line means. In fact, the "It Says, I Know, and So" strategy would do little to help students comprehend what a "Milagro killer" was, in the context of the story, let alone what it might be revealing about the brothers' relationship and how they were coping with the death of their mother—even if the students spoke Spanish. And, as we'll see in the small-group lesson that concludes this chapter, "It Says, I Know, and So" encourages students to *leave* the text precisely when they need to connect the dots within the text in order to see what lies beneath the surface.

Furthermore, one-size-fits-all strategies don't seem to take into account the fact that we infer for more than just one purpose or strategic end: We infer to pick up factual information that's not presented directly; we infer to draft an initial understanding of a single detail in a way that can sometimes lead to a hunch about the why's and how's of a text. And, as we'll see in the next chapter, we infer to interpret recurring details and patterns that we notice and track across texts. Each of these purposes requires us to attend to different aspects of the text and engage in slightly different kinds of thinking, which in turn necessitates different strategies. Because of this, we prefer to customize our instruction around inferring, offering more precise and purposeful strategies than the general reading-between-the-lines kind of talk that comes with wholesale inferring.

Rethinking our practice: *We offer students precise, customized strategies for inferring rather than a one-size-fits-all strategy.*

WE TUCK IN KNOWLEDGE ABOUT THE READING PROCESS AND
HOW TEXTS WORK THROUGHOUT OUR LESSONS

While we always think twice before giving students background information and vocabulary, considering whether they can construct it for themselves from the details in the text first, we do tuck in information about both the reading process and the way texts work throughout whole-class lessons. In this lesson, for instance, we begin with an explicit teaching point—that readers consider the significance of details by connecting what they wonder about with what they already know from the details they have noticed—and we set that within the larger purpose of reading, explaining that we do this in order to begin to see what the author might ultimately be trying to explore about people or life through this story. Then we slip in other teaching as we go. We talk to students about the placement of detail (in this case, the line of dialogue at the end of the chapter) as a way of heightening their awareness of how writers position information to intrigue us and get us thinking. We reiterate how narratives work, through scenes that often reveal information indirectly—that show, instead of tell—and through other kinds of details that show *and* tell. And we end the lesson by introducing a major teaching point about how thinking about details can lead to hunches about the text's why's and how's. In this way, the lesson unfolds like a text, burrowing deeper as it goes. And the students take a journey through the lesson, accumulating meaning both about the specific text and about how readers read.

WE CHOOSE THE LANGUAGE WE USE TO TEACH STRATEGIES
TO BEST CAPTURE THE WORK READERS DO

Throughout this lesson, you undoubtedly noticed echoes of familiar strategy instruction. The lesson is all about inferring, for instance, though that word doesn't appear. And our call for hunches is a variation on the standard call for predictions, a word that also is absent. These are deliberate choices we made—and, as you may also suspect by this point, there is purpose behind them.

While we may be splitting semantic hairs here, we believe that there is an important distinction between a prediction and a hunch. Merriam-Webster defines a hunch as "a strong intuitive feeling, especially concerning a future event or result," and relates it to words such as *hypothesis*, *supposition*, and *guess*. A prediction, on the other hand, is defined as "a declaration that something will happen in the future." Thus, by definition, a prediction is more definitive than a hunch; it is a declaration, not a supposition—and we've seen what can happen with students when they get too wedded to their declarations. A hunch, on the other hand, supports the idea that, as we make our way through a text, our understanding of it is a draft that will almost inevitably go through numerous revisions as we encounter new information and fit more pieces together. It keeps us more open and flexible, while encouraging us to read closely in order to spot and consider detail clues.

Similarly, in the last chapter, we made a deliberate decision to use the word *wonder* rather than *question* when asking students to think about what they didn't know. As with predictions, we often find that when students are asked to question as a strategy, they can produce questions that stray far from the text or questions whose answers are already known, simply to meet our request. And presenting instruction around "fat" or "thin" questions or levels of questioning—i.e., those whose answers can be found directly in the text, those that are still text-bound but require inferring or interpretation to answer, and those that reach beyond the text—doesn't always work, especially if students are asked to come up with questions as an academic exercise of the "bring-in-three-fat-and-three-thin-questions-for-homework-tomorrow" variety. In shifting our language from questioning to wondering we hope, instead, to keep our students' questions more securely tied to authentic curiosity about the territory of the text. And interestingly enough, in this lesson, when students were sticking really close to the text, questions erupted spontaneously, without explicitly being asked for or taught.

As for inferring, we will certainly introduce the term at some point, but only after our seventh graders have rolled around in the text for a good, long stretch and have a sense of what inferring actually sounds, looks, and feels like. We will also want to highlight the way the word refers to a spectrum of mental operations—from "inferring" the gender of a character by noticing a pronoun woven into a scene, as we did in the last chapter, to "inferring" an interpretation of a text's theme by noticing and tracking patterns that change, as we'll explore in the next one—so that the students get a feel not just for the means, but the end, what those means allow us to do as readers.

Finally, we want to help students see how what we do as readers is connected to the way that texts are put together, with inferring being the tool that readers use to understand what writers might be showing and telling us through the

Rethinking our practice:
We've reconsidered the language we use to teach strategies to better capture the authentic work readers do and make difficult concepts more accessible.

details and structures they've deliberately chosen. To make these concepts accessible and visible, we prefer to use kid-friendly language, with academic vocabulary introduced later on when students have some actual experience to attach the term to.

WE CREATE ANCHOR CHARTS TO HELP STUDENTS HOLD ONTO THE PROCESS OF MEANING MAKING

At the end of the lesson, we create another chart to help students hold onto the particular kind of inferring work they've done here (Figure 4–4). Unlike the charts we've made so far, which record the specific ideas and details students are noticing in the read-aloud text, this chart names the strategies students used to dig deeper into the text in a way that promotes the transfer of the process to other texts the students will read. For this reason, we call this an anchor chart; it is one that will remain up in the room until every child has internalized the thinking and no longer needs its support. We construct the chart with the students, enlisting their help in naming the steps and drawing on the language we used in the lesson. We prefer constructing charts this way over providing students with a ready-made list of strategies readers use to infer, because we believe it is more meaningful to have it come directly out of the class's actual experience. Similarly we prefer to introduce skills such as these with texts the students are already engaged with, rather than with passages taken out of context or isolated for skill practice. It's another way to keep the learning real, though as seen in our next section, we do provide students with additional opportunities to practice this vital skill on shorter texts.

Rethinking our practice: *We create classroom charts that don't just list* what *readers do but describe* how *they do it.*

Making Every Student's Thinking Visible

HELPING STUDENTS CONSIDER THE SIGNIFICANCE OF DETAILS THROUGH A STRATEGY GROUP

For many students, considering the significance of individual details by inferring, and then using that inference to develop a hunch or a line of inquiry about the

Digging Deeper into Books
Strategies We Use to Think About Our Wonderings and Develop Hunches
▶ Look closely at our wonderings for questions that remain unanswered (those that come from the end of a chapter are particularly good to explore).
▶ See if a wondering could be connected to something we already know or to another wondering–or even the title.
▶ See if those connections give us hunches about the answer to any of our wonderings.
▶ Keep an open mind as we read on, looking for new details or clues to add to our thinking.
▶ Be prepared to revise our hunches as we get new information, because that's what readers do.

Figure 4–4. Co-created anchor chart on how readers infer

text's why's and how's, is the single most challenging work for them to grasp and develop as readers. And so, we frequently bring children together to practice this kind of thinking in what can be seen as a variation on a traditional strategy group. Like our stepped-up lesson in the last chapter, we want students to not just practice a strategy but to use it to reach an "aha" moment, so that they can fully experience how the strategy enables them to "see" something that they hadn't before. In this way we aim to tie the strategy of inferring to its strategic end—insight—and make something that's invisible in texts, such as the significance of details, visible for every student.

We share an example of this more precise kind of strategy lesson here, using an excerpt from Patricia Reilly Giff's *Fish Face* (1984) with a small group of fourth-grade students (Figure 4–5). As readers, we can see in this passage that much information about the characters is conveyed through the details. We get a first-impression sense of each of the characters as well as some initial thoughts about how they feel about the other, which in turn signals some problems. Our goal is to help students first notice these details and then think about their possible significance by connecting them to other details in the text in a way that allows them to have some hunches about the bigger why's and how's that the author might be laying into place.

Just then the classroom door opened. It was the principal. There was a girl with him.

She had curly brown hair and little red ladybug earrings.

Emily pushed at her own straight-as-a-stick hair. She flicked at her ears.

No earrings.

Plain.

Her mother said she couldn't have her ears pierced until she was ten. At least.

Maybe she should ask again. Beg.

"We have a new girl," the principal said. "Here from Florida . . . This is Dawn Bosco."

Ms. Rooney said, "Let's find a seat for you, Dawn."

Emily raised her hand . . .

Ms. Rooney looked at Emily and nodded. "Sit next to Emily," she told Dawn.

Emily looked up at Ms. Rooney.

She was the best teacher in the whole school.

She was probably the best teacher in the whole world . . .

Dawn came down the aisle. She slid into the desk next to Emily.

While Ms. Rooney talked with the principal, Dawn began to unpack her schoolbag. She pushed Emily's notebook a little so it wasn't on her desk.

"You have a pretty name," Emily whispered.

Dawn didn't say anything. She took a notebook out of her schoolbag. It was pink with flowers on it.

> *Then she unpacked her pencil box. It was the kind with draw-ers. Inside were paper clips. And erasers. And little round things to stick on looseleaf.*
>
> *It had everything. Even a blue pencil with a pink tassel.*
>
> ---
>
> *At last Dawn looked at her. "What's your name again?"*
> *"Emily."*
> *"Oh," Dawn said.*
> *Emily waited for Dawn to say she had a pretty name too.*
> *Instead, Dawn said. "My middle name is Tiffanie."*
> *Lucky.*
> *"That's nice," Emily said. . . .*
> *"What's your middle name?" Dawn asked.*
> *Emily didn't answer at first. She didn't have a middle name.*
> *Dawn began again. "What's—"*
> *"Theresa," Emily said. "Emily Theresa Arrow."*

Figure 4–5. Excerpt from *Fish Face* by Patricia Reilly Giff (pp. 11–14) for strategy group lesson on noticing details and considering their significance

As in our previous stepped-up lesson, we begin by sharing with the students what we know about how texts work and how that's connected to the specific work readers do that we'll be practicing today. Thus, we introduce the lesson by explaining—or, if we're working in tandem with a read-aloud, reiterating—that writers use details to not only help us picture a scene in our minds but to convey what kind of people the characters are and how they relate to each other and deal with whatever problems they seem to have. Thus they choose their details very carefully, showing us what the characters look like, what they do and think and say in a way that also tells us something about them. And our job as readers is to think about what those details might be revealing. Additionally, we say, writers do that slowly, over the course of the story, so readers have to put details together, or connect them, in order to "see" what an author might be revealing.

To do that, the students will need to read slowly, thinking about each detail and how it might connect with others to reveal something about the characters. In this way we hope to additionally show them how readers develop a first-draft understanding not just about what's happening but why. They'll then revise, sharpen, and hone these drafts as they encounter more details. To aid them in this work, we provide each student in the group with a copy of the text, which we've chunked into shorter sections to support a slower, closer read, along with a pencil to underline any details they notice that they think might be telling them something—even if they're not absolutely sure what that something is.

As they read the first section in this slowed-down fashion, most of the children notice that the author has given us details that describe both characters' hair and ears, and now that they're paying more attention to these details, they're able to take the next vital step and "see" that the author is deliberately comparing the two of them, much as we immediately realized that Susan Marie Scavo was comparing and contrasting two different people's perceptions in her poem, "Food. Music. Memory." Once the students have noticed these details, we ask them if they have any ideas about what the author might be trying to tell us about these characters by choosing to show us this. Most retell to us the physical differences—that Dawn has pierced ears and Emily doesn't—but don't yet reach an inference.

As we make our way to the next section, continuing to read slowly to notice the details, the students again retell what the text says, that Emily is raising her hand and looking at Ms. Rooney. We ask them again to tell us if they have any ideas about why the author is giving us that information. Using what we assume they'd previously been taught about text-to-self connections, several students speculate that she might be wanting to go to the bathroom.

We ask students to hold that idea in their minds as a draft and then see if it might make sense once we connect it to other details. "Oh," one student says as she read through the section, "she wants Ms. Rooney to let Dawn sit next to her."

"Why did you change your mind?" we ask, and she points to the part where Ms. Rooney lets Dawn sit next to Emily. "What do you think?" we ask of the others.

All of the students agree that Emily wants Dawn to sit next to her and so we notice and name how they made that inference: "You noticed a detail, held a hunch about what it might mean in your brain, and then tried to connect it with other details the author gave. Connecting the details helped you think back and revise your hunch."

We ask them to do the same work—connecting details—with other details they notice in the text. Encouraging them once again to ground their thinking only in the information in front of them—and not make connections that might lead them to speculate beyond what the author's provided—one student points to the detail about Emily believing that Ms. Rooney is the best teacher in the world and infers that it's because she's acknowledged Emily's raised hand and has told Dawn to sit next to her. Other students add on and conclude at the end of that section that Emily might want to be Dawn's friend.

These students have done good work but we know it's just a start, so we challenge them: "How does your idea about Emily wanting to be Dawn's friend fit together with some of the details about the earrings you noticed?" The students look at the text again.

"Maybe she's jealous," says one student, and when we ask how she got that idea, she surprises us by pointing not to the details we've already talked about but to some others that we haven't yet talked about as a group—the description about Dawn's notebook and pencil box.

Another student points to Emily's whispered comment to Dawn as another detail that connects to her wanting to be Dawn's friend. Additionally, one student notices the detail about how Dawn doesn't say anything back to Emily when Emily talks to her. Demonstrating how quickly this work helps students get the hang of inferring, this student concludes, "Maybe she's shy." But another disagrees: "She seems a little mean," and points to the detail about Dawn pushing Emily's notebook off the desk.

At each step along the way, students have different "aha" moments as they realize that connecting details helps give them more than factual information about who's doing or saying what. Each of them is inferring and demonstrating how readers begin to construct first-draft impressions of characters.

But we haven't finished yet. Nowhere is this work more needed than in the last section when students must first infer that Emily is lying when she tells Dawn her middle name and then must consider why she would do that. Unaccustomed to reading between the lines—and not used to connecting details, even when they're almost side by side—some students need a few minutes to reread, as well as an enthusiastic reminder about what this work has already enabled them to do, before they grasp the fact that Emily has lied. In fact, a few students figure this out before the others. The "oh's" they exclaim when they finally "see" this are those satisfying sounds of insight and are followed by other students in the group eagerly seeking out the textual clues. Each student is beginning to make sense of two big inferences they have made from all the details in this passage: that Emily is jealous of Dawn and that she wants to be Dawn's friend. Many students leave the group wanting to keep reading the book in order to find out the questions they next wonder: Will Dawn eventually find out that Emily's lying and, if so, how will that affect their relationship? And is Dawn just shy, or is she really mean? And how will that impact the friendship that Emily seems to want?

WHAT THIS LESSON ALLOWS STUDENTS TO DO

Here we see students reaping the benefits of reading more closely and carefully, connecting detail to detail to infer both what is actually happening in the scene—e.g., that Emily is lying—and what's going on at a deeper level, inside and between the characters. The students also move here from the literal to the abstract as they "see" the significance of the details. Thus a flick of an ear signifies envy, a lack of response either shyness or cruelty. These readers will have to read on to learn more, honing and revising their thinking as they go. But when they do, they'll be reading forward not just to find out what happens next but to think about the why and the how. And they'll slip fewer stitches because of their new heightened awareness of the role details play. Thus, they'll be fully "in" the text in a way that better positions them to access whatever nugget of wisdom about people or life the book might contain. And while they might need the occasional reminder to slow down and consider details and how they may be connected until doing so becomes second nature, they'll be reading with more concentration and engagement than they had before, knowing that they're capable of genuine insight, with the tools and experience to prove it.

Rethinking How We Teach Reading	
What We Used to Do . . .	**What We Do Now . . .**
We used to prompt and lead students to see whatever we saw in a text.	We follow students' attention and lead to help them think more deeply about what they notice in a text.
We used to plan lessons to teach standard comprehension strategies (e.g., questioning, connecting, etc.).	We plan lessons based on our assessment of the demands of the particular text we're using.
We used to frontload background information or ask the students to access their own background knowledge before reading a text as a matter of course.	We give students the opportunity–and the tools–to construct the world of the text from the details the author provides.
We used to use think-alouds to show students how readers use strategies to make meaning.	We provide students with the tools and scaffolds to construct their own meaning instead of taking on ours.
We used to offer students one-size-fits-all strategies for inferring.	We offer customized strategies for inferring based on our understanding of the different reasons readers infer (e.g., to figure out the who, what, when, and where of a text and to draft an understanding of what kind of person a character is and what kinds of problems they face).
We used to ask students to make text-to-self, text-to-text, and text-to-world connections as a matter of course.	We ask students to make connections within a text, knowing that texts are self-contained worlds that will answer many of the questions they raise.

Making It Work: Some Practical Tips for Implementation

Harnessing the Power of Small-Group and Partner Talk

In this lesson and the ones that follow, you'll see us repeatedly asking students to turn and talk with a partner or a small group of peers as a way of ensuring that everyone tries on the thinking work we're exploring that day. Asking students to turn and talk also gives us an opportunity to informally assess what the students are doing with our instruction as we circulate among groups and partners to listen. Of course, though, talk sometimes requires scaffolding, and so, while we offer some specific ways we do that in the following chapter, we offer here a few tips and pointers to get you and your students going.

▶ **We carefully consider how to pair and group students.**
Creating productive small groups and partnerships is an art more than a science, and you may have to experiment with different combinations before you find a partner or group that works for every student. Sometimes friends can work together; other times they can't. Often homogenous groups work well, though pairing heterogeneously–say, a quiet but confident reader with an outgoing struggling one–often creates win-win situations. Additionally, we move students around over the course of a year so that every student has the opportunity to both support and be supported by other students–i.e., to be both a leader and a learner. Whatever you do, rest assured that the time you spend trying to find groups and partners who can work well together will be time well spent for you and the students alike.

▶ **We create a classroom culture that values questions and flexible thinking over answers.** Unfortunately, the current climate of standardized testing, which emphasizes answers over questions, has left many students reluctant to speak unless they're sure they've got the "right" answer. To counter that, we always try to applaud students who say "maybe" and ask questions, while also acknowledging that confusion is an inevitable part of reading–in fact, it is where understanding begins. As you'll see in the next two chapters, we also carve out ample time for students to explore their thinking through talk, with a minimum amount of prompting, so that they are able to own the process and whatever understanding they arrive at.

▶ **We help students see how talk can be used to generate and deepen thinking.** As teachers, we know that talk serves two main functions: We talk to explain or demonstrate what we've already come to understand and we talk to explore and develop understanding. The Common Core State Standards acknowledge these different functions by identifying two strands in their Speaking and Listening Standards: "Presentation of Knowledge and Ideas" and "Comprehension and Collaboration." Many students, however, have had far less experience in collaborative talk than in oral presentations. To help them see the latter–and feel the power in the old adage "Two heads are better than one"– we rely once again on our ever-useful method of noticing and naming, pointing out to students, as you see both here and in the next chapters, what they did and what they were able to achieve by trading and considering each other's ideas in a way that actually grows and deepens thinking.

▶ **We hold students accountable for their talk by asking them to write and reflect.** While we try to touch base with every group or partnership over the course of a week in order to offer any needed support and formatively assess the talk, we also ask students to periodically write a one- or two-sentence summary of their talk in their reading notebooks or on sticky notes, which we add to our class charts. This not only gives us an additional assessment window but lets the students see the diversity of thinking within the community of the room.

Chapter Five

How Readers Look Closely at Patterns to Draft Understandings

What we call chaos is just patterns we haven't recognized.

What we call random is just patterns we can't decipher.

—Chuck Palahniuk

A fourth-grade teacher, whose students had recently embarked on book clubs, invited us to stop by to check in with her. She was excited by the work, and, sure enough, as we entered the room there was a palpable sense of energy and the hum of work in the air. Books were open and the students seemed engaged and on task.

"It looks like it's going really well."

"Yes," the teacher agreed. "The kids are loving their books and their groups. They're keeping up with the reading and the talk seems to be going well. But," she hesitated, "every once in a while I worry that they should be doing more—or that I should be doing more. I mean, they're doing everything they're supposed to do, but I'm not always sure they're getting as much out of their books as they could be. Maybe they're just skimming the surface."

We knew what she meant. In fact, that nagging sense that both our teaching and our students' learning fell somewhat short of the mark is precisely what led us to explore and develop the ideas in this book. But before we offered any suggestions, we asked her to say more, to give us an example of what she hoped they'd get out of their books that she feared they weren't getting.

"Well," she said, pointing to one group. They were reading Kate DiCamillo's *Because of Winn-Dixie* (2000), a story about a motherless girl named Opal whose life starts to change when she meets a stray dog she names Winn-Dixie. "The book is so simple but also really deep. It's easy to miss things. Like when I read it I was struck by the fact that Opal calls her father 'the preacher.' That seemed to say so much about their relationship, but the kids don't seem to have noticed it, and they're almost halfway through the book."

What a difficult position this teacher was in. *Because of Winn-Dixie* is a book she knows and loves dearly, but she also knows that her role as a teacher isn't to deliver her understanding of a book to her students but to help them find their own.

We asked her to tell us more about how she knew this detail was important.

"Well," she ventured, borrowing a book from a student and flipping through the pages. "First of all," she says, "Opal keeps repeating it and then she says right here,"—on page 13— "'*it's hard for me to think about him as my daddy . . . And so in my mind, I think of him as "the preacher."*'" That seems so sad to me—that she can't think of him as a father. But also," she continued, her voice filled with excitement, "it's not just Opal and the preacher. There are all these other mentions of names, too. Here—" She turned back to page 10, where Opal first names the stray dog she found (*I figured that the dog was probably just like everybody else in the world, that he would want to get called by a name . . .*). "And here," she returned to page 13, where Opal talks about her name being the same as her mother's. "Names and identity are such big issues in this story. I know I shouldn't expect my students to see the same things I do in a book, but I'm not sure how to help them see layers like this, beyond just what's literally happening." She closed the book, handed it back to the student, and gave a helpless shrug.

Once again, we found ourselves pondering what advice to give. We knew we could offer each club a variation of the small-group instruction we did in the last chapter, which might help them see the significance of individual details, the way the teacher had "seen" sadness in the detail about Opal calling her father "preacher." Yet we realized the teacher was also doing more than that. She wasn't just looking at one detail but at several, and she brought those details together in a way that enabled her to "see" what she called the "issue" of names and identity. This thinking sounded very much like understanding, where a reader begins to read beyond the literal story and into some of the deeper layers an author might be exploring throughout a text. We also realized that as she flipped through the pages of *Because of Winn-Dixie*, the teacher was demonstrating how readers do this thinking: Their minds journey back and forth across pages, connecting and accumulating details that begin to come together to reveal patterns. These patterns "show" what are often called issues, ideas, or themes that might be woven throughout the text.

We wondered: If we taught students to do this—to think across pages and recognize patterns—would they, like the teacher, begin to see beyond the literal surface of a text and into some of the ideas that might underlie the story? Would they enter the realm of understanding that we want all our students to experience?

We approached the students reading *Because of Winn-Dixie* and asked them to look back at the pages they'd read so far to see if there might be anything they noticed that kept repeating, any patterns. We gave some examples to clarify our point: "Perhaps there's a character who's always acting the same way, or perhaps there are phrases you've noticed that keep repeating."

Two of the three students opened up their books and began to flip through the pages. After a few moments, Daisy responded.

"The dog keeps smiling," she said, and when we asked her to show us where, she pointed to two pages and continued searching. "Here too." She looked up as her finger landed on another page.

Michael had been turning pages back and forth too. "The dog always wants to hear stuff," he said, and pointed to two scenes where Winn-Dixie is described as paying particular attention to humans as they talk.

Yusef, who hadn't opened his book, which made us unsure if he was really with us this morning, stated as if out the blue: "Opal is always asking the preacher about her mom."

At that, Daisy jumped in with the same sense of excitement the teacher had shown about the references to names. "And the preacher, too! He is thinking about the mom a lot!"

Although these students didn't notice the specific pattern that the teacher had, they had definitely done what she had done: noticed and connected patterns.

Of course, this was just a beginning—these students still need to explore these patterns and make sense of what they might be showing in the book—but we already knew that, going forward, their reading would be deeper and their talk more meaningful. And so we decided to leave them, flipping through the pages of their book, sharing examples and adding on to each other's before reading on to discover new patterns and continue tracking the ones they'd already found.

What We Do as Readers

Moving from the surface level of a text to those deeper layers where meaning resides requires readers not only to comprehend the words on the page, but to engage in the work of understanding by considering what the particular details of the story might be revealing about the more universal ideas or themes that the author is exploring. Yet for many of the readers we teach, this process remains a mystery. A word is just a word, a detail just a detail. None has more significance than another and none means more than it literally says. "Preacher," for instance, just means preacher; it's Opal's father's profession, not a signal about how she feels about him or how they relate to each other, and certainly not a manifestation of an idea the author might be exploring throughout the book.

As we formulate ways to teach this, we often think of the apocryphal story of the student whose teacher saw him peering closely at his book, turning it this way and that. When she asked what he was doing he replied, "I'm trying to read between the lines." To move from a word to an idea must seem to many of the readers populating our classrooms, like it does for this child, as if invisible ink is written on the pages somewhere. So how do experienced readers do it? How do we move from a detail on a page to details that permeate a book to the implications of those details? How do we move from comprehension to understanding across an entire text?

WE ENTER STORIES KNOWING THAT THE PARTICULARS
WILL YIELD UNIVERSAL UNDERSTANDINGS

As readers, we seem to instinctively know what James Joyce once said about the paradoxical nature and power of fiction: "In the particular is contained the universal" (quoted in Ellmann 1983, 505). That is, we know that when we enter a story about a specific character with unique quirks and flaws who struggles with unique trials and problems—say, a motherless girl who calls her father the Preacher and befriends a stray dog she names Winn-Dixie—we are also ultimately able to see something about people in general and the myriad ways we do or don't manage to deal with our complicated lives. Put another way, we know that the "what" of a story—its specific characters and situations—ripples with implications that reach far beyond its margins. The particular details point to something universal, to some aspect of human nature or life that the writer is exploring through the vehicle of the story. You may recognize this as what we often call in classrooms "theme," the "heart" of a story, or a text's "big ideas." But no matter what the terminology, readers know that when they crack open a book, the story they enter has a point and their job as a reader is to eventually consider what that point might be.

Interestingly enough, we do this not by actually *thinking* about theme as we make our way through a book—at least not initially or consciously. Instead we jump into the story, absorbing and experiencing it by sticking close to the particulars. We know that the particulars hold the key to understanding because we know that writers have fashioned them in order to convey, or show, meaning. To build our understanding of how this works, we can look more closely at the connections between reading and writing. Often in classrooms, we teach reading-writing connections in order to improve students' writing by studying, say, how writers use language and craft. We believe, however, that there is another fundamental reading-writing connection that supports us as readers, and that is that the way in which writers create narrative texts is connected to the way readers read them. We've seen this already as we've looked at how a writer's practice of showing, not telling, impacts us as readers. It compels us to read in a particular way, attending to those textual clues that are conveyed indirectly through scenes and to those details that are ripe with significance because they both show *and* tell. Here, we look at this same practice but how writers employ it as they compose an entire text. John Gardner, the writer and master teacher, describes this process in *The Art of Fiction* (1984, 177):

> The writer muses on the story idea to determine what it is in it that has attracted him, why it seems to him worth telling. Having determined what interests him . . . he toys with various ways of telling his story, . . . broods on every image that occurs to him, turning it over and over, puzzling it, hunting for connections, trying to figure it out, before he writes, while he writes, and in the process of repeated revisions.

On the reading side of the reading-writing equation, this means in effect that we reverse the process the writer went through in creating the story. We too brood and puzzle, turning over details and noticing connections; we pay close attention to the details chosen and arranged, knowing that they will ultimately provide glimpses of a "story idea"—the larger interests or concerns, universals, or themes that we imagine the author thought were worth exploring to begin with. But we do all of this from deep inside the story, immersed and engaged in the particulars. And this is where patterns come in.

WE READ KNOWING THAT WRITERS USE PATTERNS
TO EXPLORE AND DEVELOP IDEAS

Patterns emerge first for the writer as, through that process of trying on different details and images and discovering their connections, she settles on those that will best reveal—i.e., show, not tell—what larger interests or concerns she's trying to explore. Then she deliberately weaves them into the fabric of the story, laying them down like breadcrumbs in a forest, for her readers to follow. Of course, as we discussed in Chapter 3, when we enter a text we're bombarded with details whose meaning is far from clear. But as we gather and hold onto those details, turning the pages to find out what happens, some of those details begin to recur in a wider context throughout the story and emerge as patterns for us, as well.

This understanding of the key role patterns play in both the way writers put texts together and readers think about them seems to be another of the mental operations we do under our conscious mind's radar, without even having named it for ourselves. We can see it clearly, however, if we think back to the list of random words we handed you in Chapter 2. To make sense of it, we tried to fit the words into patterns *because*, assuming that the list was a text, we expected, unconsciously of course, to find patterns there. Thus we tried to categorize the words, to see what they had in common; we tried to make sense of their order, of what parts of speech they were, and of what they could represent. All of these were attempts to discern patterns—though ultimately we couldn't really find any because the list hadn't, in fact, been composed by a writer who had chosen and arranged those words in patterns that supported and revealed meaning.

When we finally read the poem, however, from which the words had been taken, we immediately noticed *its* patterns—the repetition of phrases, the punctuation, the pronouns, the stanzas, the trios of words. What had seemed random in the list now became, as Chuck Palahniuk says, decipherable. Recognizing these patterns enabled us to construct interpretations that assigned specific meaning to those random words, with different interpretations developing according to which of the patterns we noticed and how we weighed and measured them in relation to others. And those interpretations led us, in turn, to an understanding of the abstract ideas that lay under the text—ideas such as perception, perspective, and the legacies of childhood—along with what we thought the writer might be saying about those ideas—i.e., the theme.

The patterns in the poem were highly visible, and the poem itself was short, which allowed us to dig into the work of understanding relatively quickly. But we find that if we come to a text expecting to find patterns, we see them everywhere. We saw patterns in *Just Juice*, for instance, in all the details through which we inferred that Juice's family was poor. We saw patterns in *Fish Face* as in each paragraph we noticed Emily desiring something Dawn had—her earrings, her pencil case, her middle name. And when we offered the Winn-Dixie students an invitation to look for patterns, they, too, found them everywhere, as they noticed that Winn-Dixie *always* seemed to be listening whenever people were talking, that Opal was *always* asking about her mother, that her father thought about his wife *a lot*.

They did not, however, notice the pattern around names that their teacher had. We've seen throughout this book—in Chapter 3 when students picked up on different textual clues that supported their literal comprehension, and in Chapter 4 when students inferred significance from different details—that texts offer multiple opportunities to construct meaning. The same holds for patterns. Readers notice different patterns, and one single pattern does not necessarily hold the key to a text's deeper levels. Any of the patterns the students noticed are potentially as good a starting point for constructing an understanding as what the teacher had seen.

Similarly, every reader does not leap to make inferences about the patterns they notice at the same time. The teacher, for example, spoke to the "issue" of identity almost immediately upon noticing the repetition around names and naming, while her students kept their minds at work on noticing patterns. Many readers, not only students, stick to the particulars of the story, dwelling in the details right up till the very end, before they consider the universal.

What's important here, again as we saw in Chapter 4, is not which patterns readers notice but what they do with what they notice, which we'll explore in more depth below. First, though, let's slow down and look more closely at how readers recognize patterns in order to make explicit and visible what many readers do invisibly in their heads.

WE READ FORWARD AND THINK BACKWARD, MAKING WITHIN-TEXT CONNECTIONS TO NOTICE PATTERNS

By definition, patterns don't become patterns until you see more than one instance of something, whether it's a word, a detail, an image, or even a structural element, like the stanzas and syntax in the poem we read. Therefore, while we read on the lookout for patterns, recognizing them is something that's done retroactively, with our minds casting backward even as we read forward, connecting what we're currently reading to what we read before. When we first read a word, like *preacher*, for instance, which appears in the first sentence of *Because of Winn-Dixie*, it doesn't initially have any meaning beyond what it's literally communicating at that moment, that Opal's father is a preacher. But when we encounter it again and again, we recall its earlier mentions and read on, alert and expectant. We're now paying close attention to this odd habit Opal has of calling her dad preacher, and we begin to notice other details that seem to fit with this one: how Opal felt the need to name this stray dog the moment it crossed her path; how she ruminates about the origins of her own name. Our brains are now operating like magnets, attracting other details that we have already read and recasting them into patterns that fit with this one.

This way of reading backward is far more purposeful than the generic call to reread, which many of us tell our students so often it can feel like the "pick-up-your-socks" refrain of our teaching: something we chronically tell students to do that seems to chronically fall on deaf ears. Nor is it quite the same as going back to catch a textual clue we missed that left us unsure of where a character was or who was saying what to whom. Instead, it's more like our seventh-grade students reading *Miracle's Boys*, looking back at what they had already read in order to infer the meaning of two lines that puzzled them. They connected one detail within the text to another, which brought up a slew of why questions that helped them begin to develop first drafts of understanding.

Likewise, whether a reader physically turns back to pages already read or does so mentally, the process of recognizing patterns by reading forward and thinking backwards also involves making connections—not text-to-text, text-to-self, or text-to-world connections, but rather connections made *within* the text, one page to another, one word to another.

Recognizing patterns by making connections within the text helps readers read on with purpose and intention, noticing what there is to be noticed in a way that allows us to begin to draft understandings of the ideas the author might be showing through the story. Additionally, attending to patterns by making within-text connections allows us to see the text as a whole, with details and scenes connected to each other, which helps us begin to synthesize a text, which as we'll see in the next chapter is critical if students are to come away with a meaningful and deep understanding.

WE GLIMPSE DEEPER LAYERS BY NOTICING HOW
PATTERNS CONNECT, DEVELOP, AND CHANGE

The students in the *Because of Winn-Dixie* book club took a big step in their thinking the day they began to notice patterns. But they also did something else: They began to connect one pattern to another. We saw Daisy do this spontaneously as she realized that both Opal and the preacher were *always* thinking about Opal's mother. And just like their teacher who got excited as she saw other details that she thought were connected to her initial awareness about the word *preacher*, Daisy's thinking became electrified. By simply connecting patterns, she began to sense intention and design in what had previously seemed random, which might ultimately allow her to begin to see things that hadn't fully been apparent before, such as the possibility that Opal's mother's absence is weighing on everyone.

In this way, they were instinctively taking the first steps of what writer Norman Maclean describes in his book *A River Runs Through It* (1976): "All there is to thinking," he writes, "is seeing something noticeable which makes you see something you weren't noticing which makes you see something that isn't even visible" (p. 92). To see what isn't fully visible—e.g., whatever Kate DiCamillo might ultimately be trying to show us more universally through these recurring details about Opal's mother—the students will have to keep reading. For as we'll explore in Chapter 6, we can't fully think about what a pattern might mean or what a writer's intention might be until we come to the end of the story and learn the final outcome. But we can begin to glimpse those deeper layers by first noticing and connecting patterns and then by reading on to see how what we've noticed and connected might develop and change.

Readers know to do this, once again, because we know how narratives operate: At their most basic level, they present us with characters who develop and change as they wrestle and deal with whatever situation the writer has set up for them, which the writer shows us not only through scenes but through patterns of details. This knowledge compels us to read on carefully, attending to the small shifts in recurring details that signal that change is afoot, aware that these changes will eventually help us see whatever aspect of the human condition the writer has been exploring. Thus, in the case of *Because of Winn-Dixie*, how Opal does or doesn't keep asking about her mother as the story unfolds might ultimately show us something about how people might be able to find answers or make peace with those questions that trouble and haunt us, and how Winn-Dixie does or doesn't continue to enjoy listening to people talk will perhaps show something more universal about our need to communicate and listen. For this is the way, as James Joyce said, the particulars contain the universals.

WE DRAFT UNDERSTANDINGS BY ASKING AND POSING ANSWERS TO QUESTIONS

While the next chapter will examine in depth how we construct a final, revised understanding of what we think an author might be saying universally or thematically as we reach the end, we focus here on how readers actually begin to draft understandings the moment they start noticing patterns and questioning what they might be revealing. As we've made visible to students through our KNOW/WONDER chart, questions sit on readers' shoulders at every turn, arising naturally from our engagement with the text and our understanding that everything we encounter and notice potentially carries meaning. Here, too, we ask ourselves questions about what we've noticed, but our questions revolve around patterns. Why, we wonder, is the character always doing that? Why do these details keep appearing? Why did the writer choose to tell the story this way? What could it all possibly mean?

We believe that readers ask these types of questions so reflexively they hardly know they're doing it. When the teacher reading *Because of Winn-Dixie*, for instance, stated that identity was a big "issue" in the book, she was, in effect, answering questions she had invisibly asked herself, questions like: "What might this pattern be showing?" "How are these patterns connected?"

She answered these questions by making an inference, for what is an inference but an answer to a question—an unstated, maybe even unconscious question, but a question nonetheless? In this case, she inferred the kind of abstraction we discussed in Chapter 4 and did so by drawing on her experience (including, we suspect, her previous readings of this text) and her understanding of how the particulars of a text contain universals. As we noted before, however, even experienced readers don't consider themes or issues quite so early on. Instead they surrender to the story, living in the details. And while they, too, make inferences to answer those implicit, often unstated questions, both the questions and the inferences they make stay more rooted in the particulars as they attempt to explain why they think what's literally happening in the text is happening.

Knowing that writers explore universal human conditions through the vehicle of the story, readers often make those inferences by thinking about what they, themselves, know about human nature or behavior. As we saw in Chapter 4, they are, in a way, making text-to-self, text-to-text, or text-to-world connections. But, once again, they are making those connections for a very specific purpose. Rather than trying to get a sense of a character or their problems as revealed through specific details, readers here make connections to consider possible explanations for changes in accumulated details, or patterns, that they've noticed. Put another way, they're inferring what they think might be the underlying cause for the effects the writer is showing them, the *because* that answers their *whys*. And in that quest to find some explanation for what they see happening in the text, some readers will even go beyond what they know to entertain a possibility about people or life that they've never considered before, which is one of the big pay-offs for reading.

Of course, students don't always bring the same understandings and experiences to the texts they read—nor do they have to. As we'll see in the following lesson, there's a spectrum of inferences students make, with some digging into those deeper layers and others remaining on the surface, with inferences that feel more like traditional predictions. But no matter what we initially infer as we attempt to answer the question of what the patterns we've noticed might be showing us, we must read on to see how what we've noticed develops and evolves, knowing that *answer* is almost too strong a word. Our inferences at this point are more like the hunches we explored in Chapter 4 than answers. They are drafts of understanding that will undergo many revisions before our thinking is done. And we must, as both readers and teachers, trust that the process will allow everyone to reach those deeper levels, regardless of what kind of inference they make in their early drafts.

To demonstrate what this can look like in classrooms, we share here a string of lessons in which students begin to actively construct understandings from the patterns they notice. To support them in this, we facilitate experiences that allow them to see and do the following:

* Read forward and think backward

* Make within-text connections to notice patterns

* Track patterns to see how they may be connecting, developing, or changing

* Ask and draft answers to questions about what those patterns might be showing.

What This Sounds Like in Classrooms

In a fifth-grade classroom in Brooklyn we were reading aloud Patricia Reilly Giff's *Pictures of Hollis Woods*, the book whose opening we assessed in Chapter 2. As you may recall, Hollis is a feisty character who's been bounced from one foster home to another and whose often defiant and belligerent behavior belies a deep and secret longing for a home and a family of her own. The students had reached a point in the book where it seemed possible that Hollis may finally get her wish. She is living with an old woman named Josie who, like Hollis herself, is an artist, and she seems to be settling in. Yet frequently she thinks about another family she lived with, especially their son Steven and their mountainside home called the Branches, which she ran away from for reasons that haven't been disclosed yet.

When we first started this read-aloud, we had established the use of the KNOW/WONDER chart (see Chapter 3) but were now about a third of the way through the book. We were writing fewer entries down on the actual chart and doing more of the work orally. Additionally, students were keeping their own charts in their reading notebooks, writing down some of the things they noticed or were wondering. Not surprisingly, many of the entries in their KNOW columns were expressed as "always" or "never" statements. These were clues that the students were beginning to recognize patterns. We knew, therefore, that it was time to notice and name their thinking. We introduced the concept of patterns as we had with the book-group reading *Because of Winn-Dixie*, telling the class that writers often circle around a handful of ideas about people and life in their books, which we can begin to get a sense of by noticing details, actions, and images that are repeated in ways that form patterns. We then shared that they, in fact, had already done this when they noticed that Hollis was *always* hearing Steven in her head and that she was *always* talking about the mountain. They'd even noticed a pattern about how the book was structured: that every chapter begins with an italicized passage about one of Hollis' pictures.

Our KNOW/WONDER chart subsequently began to focus on keeping track of the patterns the students were noticing and what they were wondering about those patterns. In Figure 5–1 we have culled some of these patterns from our class charts and some from our students' reading notebooks.

What We Know	What We Wonder
Hollis is always talking to Steven in her head.	Why?
Josie is always carving wood.	Is this why Hollis gets along with her, because they're both artists?
Hollis never wants to go to school.	Is she going to get in trouble for that?
Every chapter begins with a section about Hollis' drawings that's written in italics.	Why? And are all of them written before Hollis moved in with Josie?
Hollis always talks about the colors she uses in her drawings.	
Hollis always mentions the mountain.	Did something bad happen there?

Figure 5–1. KNOW/WONDER chart reflecting some of the "always" or "never" statements that students noticed as they read the early chapters of *Pictures of Hollis Woods*

As we looked over these charts, we thought about our next steps. We considered asking these students to jump right into answering some of the why questions that had bobbed up in the WONDER column. But reflecting back to the fourth-grade teacher flipping through the pages of *Because of Winn-Dixie*, we hesitated. What seemed to electrify her thinking was not answering any questions she might have been posing—at least not right away—but dwelling with one pattern, noticing how it evolved over the text, and connecting it with another. That simple act—staying in the world of the text and noticing more deeply—took her to a more complex plane of understanding from which she could then posit some interesting interpretations. We therefore knew that if we wanted each of these fifth graders to do rich work around understanding we would first have to set up opportunities for them to notice and connect patterns.

> **What we do as teachers:**
> *We plan for authentic reading experiences within an instructional frame.*

SETTING UP STUDENTS TO NOTICE PATTERNS MORE DEEPLY

We thought that this would take several lessons, but because we had already introduced patterns to this class by explicitly naming the fact that they often allow readers to glimpse ideas and themes that authors are exploring, we picked up from there.

"Authors," we said, "choose details that help support some of the ideas they're exploring. For example, I could be writing a story about my first day of teaching. But the details I choose are going to tell the reader different things about that day. I could choose to spend a lot of time talking about how carefully I got ready that day—how my hair looked just right and I was wearing new shoes and a new skirt—and then how hard it rained and I didn't have an umbrella and I was soaked by the time I got to school. That would be telling the reader something different than if I focused on details about my students and how eager they were to please me that day—how beautiful their smiles were and how forcefully they raised their hands. And all of those would be saying something different than if I focused on the lesson that I planned—and planned and planned and planned—and how awful it turned out to be.

"As readers, therefore, we can begin to glimpse some of the ideas that a writer might be exploring by looking more deeply at the details she's chosen and seeing how those details fit into patterns. We're going to work on this for several days, but today we're just going to look more closely at one pattern, just to see what we can notice about it."

We chose the first pattern the students had noticed as a class: *Hollis is always talking to Steven in her head.* We wrote this sentence on a new piece of chart paper, and then opened *Pictures of Hollis Woods* to the page where the students first recognized this as a pattern and wrote the specific quotation that showed us that on the chart: "And I knew what Steven would be saying, *What are you doing, Hollis?*" (p. 25).

"Today we're going to track this pattern by opening the book and trying to find those earlier pages where Hollis said similar things. This is going to help us notice this pattern more closely so we can see if we can glimpse any hints about some ideas that the author might be showing us through the pattern."

We then demonstrated how to do this work, turning back to page 1 of the book and running our finger over the words, miming the act of skimming, in order to find the other times that Hollis talked to Steven in her head. We found our first example on pages 4 and 5, read the sentence out loud, and placed a sticky note on that page.

We then asked students to work with their partners, finding other examples on subsequent pages. We handed each partnership some sticky notes and asked them to mark the pages they found. After about three minutes, they shared out and we charted what they noticed (Figure 5–2).

We then organized the students into groups of three and asked them to talk about the pattern we had just tracked. "Reread each entry on the chart," we said, "and turn back to the pages in the book. Talk with each other about anything you notice."

As we checked in on the small groups, looking for opportunities to notice and name what kinds of talk they did and what that allowed them to do, one group seemed at a loss: "What do you want us to talk about?" they asked. "What do you want us to do?" We were tempted to deliver a more prompted question, such as "What do you think this pattern might mean?" or "Why is the author establishing this pattern?" but we recognized that these were the very students who were used to *receiving* meaning rather than *constructing* it. We held firm to our belief that these were the students who most needed to see that they could make something with what they noticed. We therefore bit our tongues and repeated our initial instructions, to reread the parts and talk with each other about what they noticed.

What we do as teachers: *We try to scaffold deep thinking rather than prompt it.*

Pattern (or "Always" Statement) We Notice	Where It Occurs
Hollis is always talking to Steven in her head (first noticed on p. 25: "And I knew what Steven would be saying, *What are you doing, Hollis*?")	pp. 4–5 "*Don't think about it*, Steven said in my head." p. 11 "And in my head I told Steven, *I may just stay for a while.*" p. 20 "*Too bad you don't have your drawing box*, I imagined Steven saying, *all those yellows and blues.*" p. 22 "That's what Steven would say. *You could tell her a story about that, couldn't you?*"

Figure 5–2. Making backward thinking visible by tracking one pattern in *Pictures of Hollis Woods* in order to set up students to notice more deeply

"Well," Jayden started tentatively after looking at the pages that were marked, "sometimes she's talking to him but sometimes he's talking to her."

"Yes!" we reassured the group. "That's just the kind of thing you might notice and talk about, how the pattern might be slightly different on different pages."

Karim then said, "I think Hollis likes Steven." We briefly considered steering the conversation back to Jayden's observation but waited to see how the group would respond.

"I disagree," Michelle said. "She seems sad every time his voice comes in."

"But he's showing off and stuff," said Karim, flipping to an earlier page that hadn't been marked. "I think they're going to hook up."

"But she doesn't live with him anymore. This is the past, remember?" Michelle argued. "Also, it says he felt like a brother to her. Remember when she was drawing him?"

"Yeah," said Jayden, "and when he gave her the bigger piece of the candy bar."

"He kind of gives her, like, advice too. She respects him. But no one else," Michelle continued.

"She always lies and calls everyone names."

"Yeah. 'Stucco Lady.' 'Mustard Lady,'" noticed Karim.

"She didn't give Steven a nickname."

"Or Josie."

"Maybe she's going to end up staying with Josie."

"Maybe she'll stop looking up to Steven. Maybe Josie will replace Steven in her head."

"Maybe she's going to start making her own decisions."

"Maybe they'll hook up."

NOTICING AND NAMING WHAT THE STUDENTS DID

As we listened to this group we were glad we hadn't prompted a specific question. These students were using their talk in so many different ways— to help clarify some points of literal comprehension, to draft hunches about where the story was going to go, and to draft hunches about some of the internal changes Hollis might experience. But mostly what we saw was exactly what we had hoped to, that in talking about one pattern this group began to see other patterns that they hadn't fully recognized before. They realized, for example, that Hollis always lies and always calls people names; they also realized that she hadn't given Steven or Josie a nickname. Connecting these patterns helped them grow and deepen ideas. By noticing more deeply they had, indeed, begun the process of drafting understandings from the particulars in the text.

What we do as teachers: *We trust student talk around texts to support our thinking goals.*

We reconvened the class to highlight the thinking this group had done and incorporate it into our class charts:

"In books, ideas are invisible, but patterns are visible. Exploring and connecting patterns helped this group get glimpses of some of the ideas the author might be layering into the story so far."

To help students visualize this and be able to apply it to other reading experiences, we created a new chart. It builds on the KNOW/WONDER chart, with an additional column added to more accurately reflect the thinking we saw our students doing and that readers typically do as they begin to see connections between what they notice (Figure 5–3). In the KNOW column, we wrote down the pattern the class had initially noticed; in the middle column we listed the other patterns that Michelle, Karim, and Jayden had connected to the initial pattern as they talked; and in the third column we wrote down some of the ideas they articulated from making these connections. We depicted this thinking as an addition problem, with the patterns coming together to equal what we called an "idea." Much as we did with our seventh graders in *Miracle's Boys*, we chose to posit these ideas as new questions so that students would continue to think as readers who were drafting and revising rather than as readers who had already figured something out.

What We Know (Patterns We Notice)	Other Patterns This Might Connect With ___ + ___ + ___	What We Wonder (Ideas These Connections Might Be Showing) = ____ ?
Hollis is always hearing Steven talk in her head.	Hollis always nicknames people. Hollis doesn't give Steven a nickname. Hollis doesn't give Josie a nickname.	Does Hollis like Steven as a boyfriend? Does Hollis respect Steven as a brother? Is Josie going to become more important to Hollis than Steven was? Will Hollis learn how to make her own decisions and not depend so much on others?

Figure 5–3. A revised KNOW/WONDER chart focused on connecting patterns to think about possible ideas being shown

You'll notice that not all the "ideas" expressed in the WONDER column are what we would typically think of as "big ideas" or "themes." Some of them, such as the ones about the boyfriend or brother relationship Hollis has with Steven, are more inferences about one strand of the story or one aspect of a character. We knew that, as we kept reading, these students would be noticing more and therefore these inferences would take into account more patterns that extended into the farther reaches of the book. For now we were content that we had enabled all students to take a big step toward becoming aware of how readers move from something that is visible in a text to something that

is invisible. We planned on keeping the chart up as a model for the thinking we wanted everyone to continue doing even as we pushed into deepening and refining the ideas they were beginning to glimpse.

What we do as teachers: *We teach students to construct ideas, not just identify them.*

SETTING STUDENTS UP TO DRAFT UNDERSTANDINGS

As soon as students began to notice and connect patterns, they began to notice that some of the patterns were changing. This did not surprise us, because we know that noticing and connecting leads to deeper noticing. But just as we did when we had students tracking patterns, we wanted students to slow down their thinking and examine more purposefully the changes they noticed. Therefore, we used the same techniques we used in our previous lesson to help students think back over pages they'd already read to notice more deeply around changes in patterns. Once again we used the pattern we were following in class to help set up this thinking. We started by writing the changes students had already noticed in the KNOW column of a new KNOW/WONDER chart (Figure 5–4).

In addition, students were continuing to keep track of patterns in their own notebooks. One student, Jada, had been keeping track of how often colors were mentioned. We were not sure her noticings would lead to any insightful thinking beyond, perhaps, some ideas about the author's craft, but one day as we were reading aloud, we came to this line, on page 150:

> Beatrice [Josie's cousin, an art teacher who admired Hollis' drawings] was in my head again. What had she said to me one time? *"Sometimes we learn from our own drawings; things are there that we thought we didn't know."*

What We Know **(How Is Pattern Changing?)**
▶ Steven is not mentioned as much. ▶ Steven's voice grows weaker. ▶ Hollis starts talking back to Steven in her head. ▶ She's doing something wrong now. ▶ Josie's voice is mentioned more. ▶ Josie needs Hollis. ▶ Hollis has never felt needed before.

Figure 5–4. Noticings that students made about changing patterns

An amazed "Oh" escaped out of the girl's mouth. "The colors!" she exploded. The whole class looked at her expectantly and she continued: "At the beginning all her colors were dark, like gray and black. Then she started using blues and yellows and greens. I think Hollis' drawings are teaching her something."

"Can you say more about what you think they might be teaching her?" we asked.

"Maybe," she ventured, "maybe they're teaching her that she really *does* belong with the Regans. And she's only going to realize that by looking at her drawings."

In many ways, Jada's statement was a prediction—she was considering what might happen as the story proceeded—but in other essential ways it was the beginning of an interpretation: She was considering the possible significance of something that lay under the surface and connected different parts of the text. We were doubly impressed since she had done this work around a pattern that we had not initially considered and were grateful that we had class examples that modeled this thinking and also reading notebooks that allowed each student to pursue their own lines of thinking.

We thought we could use Jada's thinking to make the process of drafting interpretations explicit to all students, so the following day we gathered the students together.

"When we were reading yesterday, Jada had an 'aha' moment. A pattern she had been tracking was changing. She knew that. But she didn't know yet why the author was doing that or what it could be showing us. She was sort of holding those questions in the back of her mind. When we read that sentence about Hollis learning from her own drawings, Jada went 'aha' because it was an answer to those questions she'd been holding onto. And she used the greatest thinking word ever to talk about that answer: 'maybe.' She said 'maybe Hollis is going to learn that she belongs to the Regans after all.'

"Because we know that patterns are ways that authors show readers ideas, looking at how these patterns change over the course of a story is a way to glimpse what a writer might be saying about those ideas. To do that, readers ask themselves questions and begin to try to answer those questions."

We wrote the questions we wanted students to ask themselves in the WONDER column of our new chart (Figure 5–5). Unlike our earlier lesson where we wanted students to notice deeply before they jumped into answering why questions, we were confident now that students had already noticed deeply and therefore their answers would be more considered.

Reflecting on our practice:
What's the difference between a prompt and a scaffold? How much of what we do in the name of scaffolding is really prompting and how much does that contribute to our students' passivity as thinkers?

What We Know (How Is Pattern Changing?)	What We Wonder
Steven is not mentioned as much.	Why?
Steven's voice grows weaker.	What could author be showing us?
Hollis starts talking back to Steven in her head.	
She's doing something wrong now.	
Josie's voice is mentioned more.	
Josie needs Hollis.	
Hollis has never felt needed before.	

Figure 5–5. Using the WONDER column to ask what the author might be showing through a changing pattern

We listened in on two groups, and each had very different ideas about why Steven's voice was growing less dominant. One group thought that perhaps Steven was going to die, since they had also been following a pattern of references to a truck accident that had not yet been explained. They were connecting these two patterns to think that perhaps Hollis was beginning to feel guilty because she might have been to blame for the accident. "She didn't used to care if she did bad things, but now she does," they agreed. Another partnership similarly focused on Steven's voice being Hollis' conscience, but thought that it was weakening because they had also noticed that Hollis was growing stronger. "She trusts herself more now," they said.

We pulled the class together to give them their next instructions.

"You've done great thinking about what the author might be showing through this changing pattern, and a lot of you connected other patterns to help you answer your questions. Because we haven't finished the book, these ideas are still drafts. We might have to revise them, depending on how the rest of the story goes. So until then, let's use Jada's word, 'maybe.' Think about some of the things you talked about with your partner and draft a 'maybe statement'—what do you think this changing pattern *may* be showing us?"

We handed each partnership a sticky note on which to write their maybe statement, which they then placed in a new column of the class chart (Figure 5–6).

Though some students' maybe statements remained on the level of prediction—i.e., they were about an event only ("Maybe Steven died")—most of the thinking that emerged from the statements—about family and what being a family means, about self-acceptance, about guilt and responsibility, and learning to live with something you've done wrong—pointed toward ideas that might be layered *around* those events, in other words, understandings. Of course we still had to finish the book, which meant that every student would have more opportunities to deepen their thinking. But we were confident that being grounded in the patterns they noticed put each student exactly where they needed to be to embark on the final work of revising and refining their understandings, which we'll explore in more depth in Chapter 6.

What we do as teachers: *We empower all of our students to be strategic with what they notice.*

We ended the class by naming for these students the thinking they had done and what that thinking allowed them to do, which we additionally charted (Figure 5–7).

What We Know (How Are Patterns Changing?)	What We Wonder	What We Think (Maybe Statements)
Steven is not mentioned as much.	Why?	Maybe Hollis is learning to live without him.
Steven's voice grows weaker.	What could author be showing us?	Maybe Steven died. Maybe Hollis killed him (accidentally).
Hollis starts talking back to Steven in her head.		Maybe Steven is like Hollis' conscience.
She's doing something she knows is wrong now.		Maybe Hollis feels guilty. Maybe Hollis trusts herself more now. She doesn't need an outside voice.
Josie's voice is mentioned more.		Maybe Josie has replaced Steven in Hollis' life.
Josie needs Hollis. Hollis has never felt needed before.		Maybe Josie is her family now. Feeling needed is family love. Maybe Hollis will move on from Steven and accept her new life with Josie.

Figure 5–6. Adding on a new THINK column to draft the beginnings of interpretive, or "maybe," statements

"Each of you read the same words but noticed slightly different patterns and connected them in different ways. That is reading! Not just reading the words, but digging into them to notice how they fit together to form ideas. We don't know how this book is going to end and we don't know what ideas from it are finally going to surface or stay with us, but one of the joys of reading a good book—and reading it together—is that we can see this. You should be really proud of the reading you've just done."

We turned around to gather our things and get ready for our next class, but the students weren't going to let us have the last word. "It's kind of like a puzzle," one of them said, and we turned back to the class. "But the puzzle isn't finished yet," another student chimed in. We couldn't have said it better, and felt a piece of our own puzzle—about how to teach kids how to read more deeply—fall into place.

Digging Deeper into Books

Strategies We Use to Consider What an Author Might Be Exploring

▶ Notice patterns (such as: characters always doing, thinking, or feeling the same thing or details or phrases that get repeated).

▶ Think about how those patterns might be connected to other patterns.

▶ Track the patterns to see if any of them are changing.

▶ Ask why questions about those patterns, and develop hunches and maybe statements to answer our questions.

▶ Talk with each other to continue to develop and refine our understandings.

Figure 5–7. Co-created anchor chart on how to consider possible emerging themes

What We Do as Teachers

WE TEACH STUDENTS HOW TO CONSTRUCT IDEAS
FROM TEXTS, NOT JUST IDENTIFY THEM

We believe that readers make meaning of texts from the words up. This means we read words that come together to reveal ideas. Much of the teaching we see belies this process, asking students instead to come up with ideas first and then identify the particulars that match. Students are taught, for example, to identify conflicts or character traits, problems and solutions, themes, or social issues. They are then asked to find evidence to support those ideas. Such tasks may work as assessments of thinking already done—for example, the Common Core State Standards expect sixth-grade students to "[d]etermine a theme or central idea of a text and how it is conveyed through particular details"—but more often than not such tasks are passing for instruction, particularly as students move up in grades. In fact, often the only instruction we see students receiving around reading is to "determine" or "identify" and then "prove" or "provide evidence" for their thinking. This mistakenly conveys to students that meaning is simply "found" or just "is," which leaves them playing a kind of Pin the Tail on the Donkey game as they read—blindly trying to identify something that has yet to be made real to them. As we know, some of them get it but many others don't, and educators are left wondering why.

What we need to teach is that reading is an act of accumulation, that meaning grows out of words that we begin to fit into patterns that we then connect and actively construct into ideas. In other words, we read from the inside out. Nowhere is this more important to make visible for our students than when we move from comprehension to understanding, from the particulars of a text to the ideas that underlie those particulars. If students can learn the mind-work involved in this step they will learn to read more deeply, which in turn will allow them to pick up on increasingly subtle textual clues that will refine their interpretations over time. We know that this process pays off—in the engagement and empowerment of our students, but also, purely and simply, in their ability to read. When students can see the raw materials that go into constructing interpretations and can see the process by which those raw materials come together toward meaning, they are surely reading.

WE PLAN FOR AUTHENTIC READING EXPERIENCES
WITHIN AN INSTRUCTIONAL FRAME

Teaching students to "construct" rather than "identify" has broad implications about how we design and deliver instruction. *How* we teach has everything to do with *what* we teach. As we began to realize this, we recognized in our own teaching how often we steered students' eyes to clues we were noticing that contributed to *our* understanding. We would be doing a read-aloud and pause dramatically at the places that *we* considered important; we would preplan lessons with specific questions we wanted students to consider at specific places in texts; we would deliver minilessons modeling what to notice in particular texts and where and when. How could we continue to teach in these ways if we believed that the process of making meaning was a vital part of the meaning itself?

In *Choice Words*, Peter Johnston discusses alternate instructional frameworks, in particular ones that set students up to be problem-solvers. "We hear a lot about teaching children strategies," he writes, "but we often encounter classrooms in which children are being taught strategies yet are not being strategic" (p. 31). Setting up problem-solving scenarios "requires setting children up to generate strategies, then reviewing with them, in an agentive retelling, the effectiveness of the strategies they generated . . ." (p. 31). This, he states, allows them to develop agency, which is essential if they are to transfer the skills and strategies we are trying to teach.

As reading teachers trying to teach within this framework, we see our role as one where we facilitate experiences that allow our students to figure out texts, to problem-solve within them. We then try to notice and name what they did, how they did it, and what that allowed them to do (the "agentive retelling" Johnston refers to). You saw us attempt to do this with Michelle, Karim, and Jayden as well as with Jada. Our teaching in these cases came out of the problem solving we saw these students doing and our retelling of what we noticed.

We think of planning instruction around this framework as a little like planning a road trip. We know our destination and we know the route we're going to take to get there, but we don't know exactly what the journey will look like, what we'll see, or where we might stop along the way. If we knew everything before we embarked, there'd be no point to the trip. If we knew nothing—if we hadn't done any planning whatsoever and didn't have a map—we might never reach our destination.

To help us plan these experiences, we therefore articulate for ourselves our endpoints—in this case that students deepen what they notice in texts and use that to begin to draft understandings. We then set up structures that allow students to do this work while we listen in. It's important to note here that we are not listening for specific thoughts or fishing for particular interpretations; rather we are listening for thinking made visible to us through thoughts. Therefore, as we embark on our plan, we recognize that although we don't know the specific thoughts that students will have about the books we teach, we are aware of the thinking we hope to facilitate—our road map—and pay careful attention to evidence of that as we teach. Words like *always, never,* or *sometimes* tell us that students are thinking across pages. *I think* and *maybe* are clues that students are drafting ideas about texts. *Oohs* and *ahhs* tell us that students are putting the puzzle pieces together.

This helps assure us, and helps us assure teachers in turn, when we are faced with students who still seem to "not get it," students who may not talk well with each other, or who continue to shrug, or who tend not to say anything marvelous. We are in classes with students who behave like this every day: These were the book-club students in our fourth-grade class, and Michelle, Karim, and Jayden in our fifth. What these students have taught us is that when they are assured that a teacher is not looking for a particular answer but rather looking for thinking—when they come to trust that we are not hoarding the answers, waiting to spring them on the students like a trap, but instead truly valuing their thinking—they will rise to the occasion. Teaching students the power of constructing something with what they notice teaches students to be strategic. In turn, we, as teachers, need to be strategic, making sure that the reading opportunities we provide give students the time and space they need to develop and grow their thinking.

Rethinking our practice:
We know the power of reading comes from constructing meaning, and we put this goal at the front and center of our teaching.

WE TRY TO SCAFFOLD DEEP THINKING RATHER THAN PROMPT IT

Because we want these thinking experiences to be genuine, we need to pay attention to when we might be prompting thinking and when we are actually scaffolding thinking. You saw us struggle with this in the initial lesson around tracking patterns with Michelle, Karim, and Jayden. We know that although some students ask why questions without prompting, many others do not. We believe that asking and posing answers to why questions is an essential step in moving from the concrete to the abstract in texts and where some students zoom ahead into the territory of understanding while others are left peering mystified at the page. In the past we tended to "solve" this problem by peppering why questions into our conversations with students, either in whole-class discussions or while talking to individual students about their independent reading: "Why did the character do that?" "Why did the character say that?" "Why do you think the author put that in?" We began to notice, however, that students weren't internalizing the thinking that these questions were meant to elicit. We often got the usual range of answers: the usual students jumping immediately to insightful thinking while the usual others shrugged, become disengaged, or grasped at canned language, such as "Because it's interesting" or "Because it keeps you reading."

In the fifth-grade class we illustrate in this chapter, we were afraid that prompting why questions early on in the reading process would result in similarly shallow answers, reinforcing the passive behavior we noticed in many of these students. With Peter Johnston's instructional framework in mind, we thought that we first needed to provide students with more opportunities to be strategic—that is, to notice deeply and *do* something with what they noticed. Over time, as students experienced this, we felt more comfortable asking them to answer why questions that we asked, as you could see in the lesson on drafting understandings, and that we would not be short-changing or undermining our students' strategic experiences, but rather supporting and reinforcing them (Figure 5–8).

Rethinking our practice:
We pay attention to whether our prompts are inadvertently keeping students from internalizing the thinking work we want them to do as readers.

A Prompt . . .	A Scaffold . . .
Leads students to notice what the teacher notices	Guides students to become aware of what they notice
Leads students to draw the same conclusions as the teacher from what they notice	Honors the conclusions students draw from what they notice
Does the thinking for the students	Allows students to do the thinking for themselves
Solves the problems for students	Facilitates problem solving
Teaches the text	Teaches the thinking around the text

Figure 5–8. Reflecting on the differences between a prompt and a scaffold

WE TRUST STUDENT TALK AROUND TEXTS TO
SUPPORT OUR THINKING GOALS

Talk is one of the best ways to teach students that understanding is construct-ed rather than identified or found, because they can see how others construct different interpretations from the same words. We tried to emphasize this in the lesson on drafting understandings, using talk as a way to clarify and deepen our students' thinking and not just as a demonstration of finished thinking. In this way the instructional framework we set up aims to facilitate reading *and* talking experiences. Our role as teachers, then, is to notice and name the thinking engendered not just by an individual, as we did with Jada, but by a group through their talk, as we did with Michelle, Karim, and Jayden.

So what do we do if our students don't talk or if their talk doesn't accomplish the goals we envision? As with all of our teaching moves, we rely a great deal on approximation and move our students incrementally from there. Listening is the tool we rely on the most to help us do this. We listen carefully for evidence of thinking and not just for brilliant thoughts. And we are patient—or rather we try to be. When we first sat down with Michelle, Karim, and Jayden, for example, we wanted to jump in to "correct" their talk, to steer it to be more accountable and focused, but when we let it wander, as it did, we were able to see what it ac-complished for those students. When we named those accomplishments back to them, their sense of agency increased, which not only improved their ability to think around a text but also improved their vision of what talk could accomplish for them—clarify and deepen their thinking.

WE EMPOWER ALL OF OUR STUDENTS TO BE
STRATEGIC WITH WHAT THEY NOTICE

As we mentioned earlier, there are many, many patterns at play in books, some subtle and some right on the page, some that require inferring and some that don't, some about obvious aspects of texts and some not. The students in the fourth-grade book club, for example, noticed patterns around the characters that were right there on the page, as did many of the students reading *Pictures of Hollis Woods*. Yet we also saw students discerning patterns around language, images, and structure, as well as more complex—and inferred—aspects of the character.

This assures us that all readers can at least begin the process of constructing understandings without first having to make inferences. Trusting this process and knowing that texts provide glimpses of ideas over time allows us to relax to some extent when not every student picks up on every clue. Just as we saw in Chapter 4, some readers will inevitably jump to higher levels of meaning before others. This is reflected in some of the maybe statements students created in *Pictures of Hollis Woods*. While some indeed sounded like interpretations, some were still literal predictions, just as some of the ideas that grew out of the connecting patterns work sounded more like inferences. If these ideas or maybe statements have been genuinely created through the process we've facilitated, we let all of them linger. We know that we haven't finished the text yet and all students will have more opportunities to draft and revise as we go. In addition, when we finish the book each student will be able to look back at their thinking, perhaps deepening and refining their ideas at that point. We'll look more closely at this in Chapter 6, but for now we are content that each student has done the strategic work we wanted them to: noticed patterns across pages, wondered what those patterns might be revealing, and drafted "maybe" answers to those wonderings.

Rethinking our practice: *We use every opportunity given us to teach the reader and not the text.*

Making Every Student's Thinking Visible

SUPPORTING A STUDENT TO NOTICE PATTERNS IN AN INDEPENDENT READING BOOK

We know that some patterns in books are more obvious than others and many books operate on many different levels. For example, we know in the fifth-grade class in which we were reading *Pictures of Hollis Woods* that there are many patterns around the character, but there is also a pattern in the structure. Every other chapter is in italics and describes a drawing that is a flashback from the present moments that are described in the regular chapters. As readers we notice this pattern and what literal information it conveys (a different time than the other chapters; a drawing of Hollis'), but we also have to consider how that pattern might connect to other patterns in a way that might deepen our understanding of why the author chose to write this book this way.

We were reminded of this recently while working in an eighth-grade classroom, conferring side by side with the teacher as her students were doing independent reading. We approached one girl who was reading *Identical*, one of several young adult books by Ellen Hopkins that explore controversial and mature themes, such as sexual abuse and drug addiction, that are popular with many teenage girls. As is our habit while conferring, we asked the girl to read out loud a bit from where she was in the book at that moment and then we asked her some questions about what she was thinking as she read. The book, we noticed, is told in verse and on some pages, including the one she was on, there are a few words set off in the margins, away from the main stanzas (Figure 5–9). We asked her about those words.

"Well," she replied, "the book is about identical twins. One page is from one twin's point of view and the other is from the other's. These words," she directed our attention to the ones in the margin, "are shared. They're the same on both pages." She then pointed to the opposite page where, sure enough, the exact same words were dangling in the margin.

The teacher whose class we were in looked at the student with awe and gave a self-deprecating laugh. "I never noticed that when I read the book!"

"Well, not every page is written this way," the student responded kindly. She was about a quarter of the way through the book and flipped through some of the pages she had read earlier.

We had also noticed that the girl had read these words as if they belonged to the main page—with no hesitation or parenthetical tone—and wanted to ask her about that decision.

"So with these words dangling in the margin, why did you decide to read them like they were part of the main poem?"

"Well," she replied, "they *are* part of the main poem. They make sense with the main poem, but they also make sense with the main poem on the other page."

"So what do you make of that? Why do you think the author chose to do that in this book?"

"So far the book is about these family issues," she said. "Something's going on, there's some secret, and the twins are having different reactions to it. And I think these words are kind of like the twins. They're identical, they share DNA, but they're having different reactions to these experiences."

"Oh, so you're thinking that these pages, the way they're written, are kind of echoing some of what the book's about?"

Sound Bites Bitten

Kaeligh
Having Mom Home

Mom actually cooks dinner
tonight, perhaps worried some
nosy journalist might peek
   through the window.

   Makes things easier. Makes things
    harder, like looking
through the window,

Of course, it's frozen lasagna
and bagged salad. But hey,
who's complaining?
  It's almost

  needing to see what's on the other
  side, but your eyes have to work
  too hard to reach beyond the grime.
It's almost

like we used to be, once
upon a time. If I close my
eyes. I can almost pretend
  like we're

  as hard as pretending I don't care
  if she leaves again. Almost as hard as
  sitting around the dinner table
like we're

a normal family, gathered
round the table, discussing
stuff like plays and grades,
  not unusual

  a cohesive family unit. A little
  pasta, little wine, little conversation.
  Damn little, which is
not unusual

dinner-table topics like war
chests and fund-raisers. . . .

  for the Gardella clan. What talk
  there is, of course, is election talk. . . .

Figure 5–9. Excerpt from *Identical* by Ellen Hopkins (pp. 88–89) showing the structural pattern an eighth grader noticed

"I think so, yeah. Because it's called *Identical*, so there's things that are the same, but there are some things that are not."

This girl was obviously a perceptive reader, noticing all that was to be noticed, asking herself why questions ("Why is this book written this way?") and drafting answers to those questions. We proceeded to tell her this—to retell what we had noticed she had done so well as a reader. We finished the conference by framing the work she had done, not just around the book she happened to be reading at that moment, but around all books.

"You've noticed a really subtle layer to this text that your teacher said she didn't even notice. Books are like that. They operate on lots of different levels. You noticed a pattern around how this story is told—its structure—and are making some sense of that pattern as you go along. Of course this pattern may change as you keep reading. Your ideas about it may change as well. That might be something interesting to keep track of, to see how, when you finish the book, the structure does or doesn't contribute to some of your final ideas about the book."

WHAT THIS LESSON ALLOWS THIS STUDENT TO DO

Noticing and naming is not just an instructional technique we reserve for whole-class teaching but one that we use almost every day as we sit and confer with students in their independent reading books. Having a student read to us from where they are in their book allows us to glimpse—or notice—their thinking *as* they read, not just *after*. How are they making sense of that page, that section, that paragraph? This helps us "see" the invisible thinking our students are doing as their eyes move over words. In noticing, however, we don't simply praise this student, pat her on the back, and say "good work, keep going." Rather, we try to name back to the student what we saw her doing and frame that thinking within the larger work of reading—how that thinking can help expand her understanding, not just of the book she's in at this moment but other books she'll read in the future. In that sense, even though we have focused only on a small section of text, our conference is really not about the book at all. Rather, the book has become a vehicle for us to help the student see her own thinking so she can be more purposeful, adept, and aware.

Rethinking How We Teach Reading	
What We Used to Do . . .	**What We Do Now . . .**
We used to ask students to reread to see what they missed.	We now ask students to think back to recognize patterns.
We used to think that our access to a text was *the* access to a text–and teach that.	We know that meaning is made in different ways for different readers and try to teach students to notice deeply and do something with what they notice.
We used to teach students to *find* meaning in a text.	We now teach students to make meaning in texts.
We used to teach students strategies by telling them what to do when.	We now try to teach our students to be strategic by setting up problem-solving experiences, listening carefully as they think and then noticing and naming their thinking and what that thinking allowed them to do.
We used to frontload our teaching of literary elements.	We allow understanding of literary elements to emerge as meaning emerges so their purposes and functions can be better understood.
We used to use graphic organizers that assessed student comprehension.	We now use graphic organizers that attempt to teach students how readers think in texts–and assess from there.
We used to prompt student thinking with the idea that it would help them understand.	We see that those prompts created passive thinking that students weren't internalizing, so we now try to scaffold their thinking instead.

(continues)

(continued)

We used to think that *how* we taught was disconnected to *what* we taught.	We now know that how we teach has everything to do with what we teach.
We used to think student talk in classrooms was only about engagement.	We now know that talk is an essential component in building interpretations and therefore highlight that in our teaching.

Making It Work: Some Practical Tips for Implementation
Helping Students Track Patterns

Our KNOW/WONDER chart has evolved as we have moved from the beginning to the middle of a book. Our KNOW column now looks more like a column on keeping track of PATTERNS, which means it has thinned out considerably since we first started it at the beginning of the book.

▶ We often **keep track of one pattern as a class** to serve as the model for what we want students to do on their own.

▶ We also **ask students to keep track of their own patterns** in their reading notebooks, giving them time to do this in class or for homework.

▶ You can do some **differentiation** in your class. At some point in narratives many patterns converge but we know that, at least initially, it may be enough for some students to track only one pattern at a time. Others might rise to the challenge of tracking multiple patterns.

▶ Having **class sets of the read-aloud** book is helpful during these lessons but not necessary. Other possibilities include:

  • Sharing a few copies of the text, alternating days when students have access to the text to look back at patterns they are exploring.

  • Modeling this work in a read-aloud and having students apply it in book clubs, with book partners, or in their independent reading.

  • If you have computers available in your room, students can access the text through the "Look Inside" option available on Amazon.com. They won't be able to read every page but can easily search for key words that will show them passages.

(continues)

(continued)

> ▶ We recommend **judicious use of sticky notes**, perhaps using them to help students initially mark the pages where a pattern has been found, but then having students write the page numbers down in their reading notebooks with some paraphrasing about what's happening with the pattern on that page.
>
> ▶ We also recommend **judicious use of writing time**. Mostly we want students to be reading and thinking, not copying, so we are watchful with these charts—whether we are keeping them as a class or students are keeping them in their reading notebooks—lest the tool becomes a task.

Chapter Six

How Readers Put All the Parts Together to Revise Their Understandings

*The storyteller . . . writes numbers on a blackboard, draws a line under them,
and adds them into their true but unsuspected sum . . .*

—Randall Jarrell

We are in a school meeting with a fourth-grade teacher who has been experimenting with different ways to help her students understand what she's alternately called the main idea, a big idea, or theme. "It's so hard," she says, as we pull up a chair at one of the room's round tables on which she's placed some of her students' reading notebooks and a handful of charts and graphic organizers that students have created both individually and as part of a group. "All the students can retell and many can summarize, but after that things often start to fall apart, even with my more confident readers."

"Believe us, we know," we say with sympathy. "We've been struggling with this, too, for years. Can you tell us what you've tried to do and show us what the kids have done with that?"

"Sure," the teacher says, pulling out a few of the charts, which she explains were part of a culminating project for her unit on historical fiction. She introduced the class to the genre through a read-aloud of Patricia Polacco's picture book *Pink and Say* (1994), about two boys, one white and one black, who forge a moving friendship during the Civil War. The students then formed book groups to read a historical fiction novel together. Once they finished, she asked them to create a chart that showed how they used the elements of historical fiction to strengthen their reading comprehension, with four columns respectively bearing the headings Character, Setting, Plot, and Theme.

"They did okay on the first three," she says as she sets two of the charts in front of us, one from a group that had read Patricia MacLachlan's *Skylark* (1994) and the other from students who had read Elizabeth George Speare's *The Sign of the Beaver* (1983). "But when it came to theme, I think all they did was pick up some of the words we used when we read *Pink and Say* together."

We scan the charts quickly as she speaks, with our eyes zeroing in on the last column where the *Skylark* group has written the words *bravery* and *determination* and *The Sign of the Beaver* group has put down those same words and added two more: *courage* and *friendship*.

"It's not like those words don't apply to those books," the teacher says with a sigh, "but those words alone don't really capture the richness of those books."

"No," we agree, explaining to her that single words also never capture how those books might have slightly different things to say about determination or bravery, which is always a danger when we think about themes as a single abstract word.

"Exactly!" the teacher says. "That's what I thought, too. It's like the theme was a vocabulary sticker that they put on the book. But then I thought that might have been partly due to the way I'd set up the chart. So then I tried it another way with the students' independent reading books, but I ran into problems there, too."

She explains then how, on the heels of the book groups, she decided to return to a scaffold that had helped her students earlier in the year as they worked at moving from retelling to summarizing. To show us, she pulls out some graphic organizers that we recognize immediately as a variation on a "Somebody Wanted But So" chart. These SWBS organizers ask students to get to the gist of a text by thinking about who a narrative is mostly about, what they wanted but couldn't get, and the consequences. To that, the teacher had added a second part to the "So" column that she hoped would get the students to expand their thinking about the big idea or theme beyond a single word: She asked them to consider what the "somebody" had learned.

"Some kids did a great job with it," she says. "But here's one of several where it really didn't work."

She hands us one of the organizers. It's the work of a student named Carly, who has read Charlotte Zolotow's gender-bending picture book *William's Doll* (1972), about a little boy who desperately wants a doll. He begs his father to buy one for him, but his father can't quite let go of the notion that dolls are not for boys, until his own mother, William's grandmother, helps him see that all William wants is the chance to care for something as deeply as his father cares for him. Using the chart graphic organizer, Carly summarized the book this way: "William wanted a doll but his father wouldn't buy one for him. So his grandmother did." Then under the section about what was learned, she wrote, "William learned not to whine."

"Hmm," we say, acknowledging the problem. "She seems to have forced her thinking to fit the organizer and didn't really see the connection between the parts, even though you were attempting to help her do that."

"I know," the teacher says. "So what can I do?"

What, indeed, we wonder, as the teacher's struggles force us once again to delve into the minefield of what it means to read deeply and make meaning. We will need to spend many more days in this classroom trying to replicate the work around patterns we shared in the last chapter with her and her students, along with the ideas we present in this chapter about how readers wrestle with the ends of texts and try to synthesize all the parts in order to revise their understandings to make sense of the text as a whole.

But before we pull our calendars out and begin to schedule dates, we notice and name for the teacher the thinking work that she's done, just as we do with students. She has built her instruction around her understanding of the richness and complexity of narrative texts and of how readers sometimes use literary elements to deepen their understanding. She realized, however, that the first scaffold she offered—the character, setting, plot, and theme chart—just kept the students on the level of identification, rather than understanding. To rectify that, she designed another scaffold whose purpose was to help her students see how the theme or the main idea, as shown through what was learned, was organically connected to the arc of the story though, once again, too many students still couldn't "see" that and answered the question about lessons learned in a way that seemed strangely divorced from the story—more an afterthought than a natural outgrowth. And all this led her back to the proverbial drawing board to revise and rethink her next steps, just as we've done over the years, as our thinking has evolved.

What We Do as Readers

As we travel around the country, visiting schools, we often see teachers, as we have here, working incredibly hard to teach what is sometimes called end-of-the-book work. They are trying to help students "see" those larger ideas that permeate and are woven throughout texts by authors who have deliberately chosen details and a particular story line to explore whatever nugget of the human condition they find themselves preoccupied with—in other words, the theme. As we've seen above, however, despite the effort we, as teachers, put in, students often seem to miss the mark, latching onto a single abstract word that conveys none of the complexity, nuance, or depth we know is in a text, or onto ideas that only seem tangentially connected to the actual words on the page.

So what do we draw on to do this work? What allows us to come away from a text with a deeper understanding about people and life, beyond a vocabulary word? What helps us see that "true but unsuspected sum" that lies beneath the events of a text?

WE READ FOR AUTHENTIC PURPOSES, NOT JUST TO IDENTIFY A THEME

We believe that the key to being a successful teacher of reading is to draw on our own authentic experiences and understandings as readers, and in doing so, we must acknowledge that, as readers, we never read a text to identify something as complex as a theme. That's not to say that we're unaware of the abstractions an author seems to be circling—poverty, for instance, in *Just Juice*, envy in *Fish Face*, identity in *Winn-Dixie*. We infer them through those details that both show *and* tell as we saw in Chapter 4, and in the patterns we notice and track as we saw in Chapter 5. But our goal is never to pin a single word like *bravery* or *friendship* on a text.

Instead we read for deeper reasons, to engage in a kind of conversation—or to use Louise Rosenblatt's word, transaction—with the writer, who has generously and thoughtfully shared what he's noticed about the strange, remarkable, or moving ways we deal with and stumble through life so that we, as readers, have the chance to consider whatever we think the story might have to say about those one-word abstractions or ideas. In this way, we agree with writer Janet Burroway who, in her book *Writing Fiction* (2003), suggests that "[w]e might better understand theme if we ask the question: *What about what it's about?*" (p. 357). What in particular might the story *Skylark* be saying about bravery—its causes, its effects, its different facets or complications? And what is the particular take *The Sign of the Beaver* has on friendship? In this way, we know that those abstract ideas are just the tip of the iceberg. And if we notice them, we read on, wondering and questioning how what we've noticed will or won't play out as the story unfolds.

For readers this requires a particular kind of mind-work comprising attentiveness and openness, which we attempt to promote in classrooms through the use of scaffolds such as our KNOW/WONDER chart and our emphasis on the process of drafting and revising. But we also, as teachers, need to trust that when we reframe our teaching around these larger goals—and teach the process as well as the product of reading—we'll still manage to meet the bullet points and expectations our standards and administrators require us to meet. We need to trust, as Vicki Spandel has said about writing in *The 9 Rights of Every Writer*, that

> . . . when we teach writing for the right reasons–to help our children write with passion and touch the hearts of readers–the little things tend to fall into place anyway. We get the topic sentences and details and strong verbs we hoped to see because those little things help the writer reach her loftier goal. What's more, the writer learns to care about such things, not because we said she should, but because these writer's skills took her where she wanted to go all along, to a place where her writing became powerful. (p. xiii)

Applied to reading, what this means is that we'll get the theme, the analysis, and the content of our curriculum if we show students how to read for meaning, delving into a text with their minds and hearts open to whatever a writer might be exploring. And they'll do it, not because we tell them to, but because they feel the excitement of thinking and the power of reading to inform their lives, just as real readers do. They'll do it because they'll have become active agents in the construction of their understanding of both texts and their own lives.

WE REMAIN FLEXIBLE AS PART OF OUR ONGOING CONVERSATION WITH THE WRITER

Of course, reading this way doesn't happen by osmosis. It requires our active participation as we make our way throughout the text, not just at the end, which seems to be the major problem with much of what we ask students to do. The first handful of details the writer gives us, is, in effect, the start of the conversation, and after listening and paying attention, we respond with questions and initial ideas—i.e., what we wonder and what we know or think—which we carry with us to develop, revise, and refine as the conversation continues. We saw our fifth graders doing this in the previous chapter as they noticed, connected, and tracked different patterns, revising and deepening their thinking as they went, with the pay-off being those "aha" moments when they saw how something they'd noticed in a text allowed them to see something deeper and more hidden that they hadn't noticed before.

All this requires flexibility. We have to be willing to reconsider what we've already read while remaining receptive to whatever twists and turns the writer might still have in store for us—none of which is easy. Sometimes we have to let go of old thinking, which we've become attached to, because the text takes a turn that we hadn't expected, as we'll see when we step into a fourth-grade classroom in the lesson that follows; or because we've been tracking a pattern that fades or disappears altogether, as happened in the seventh-grade class that had been reading *Miracle's Boys*. Many of those students had developed hunches and maybe statements about Newcharlie's experience in the juvenile detention home he'd been sent to. They were sure that something had happened to him there that would account for the changes his brother had noticed. But despite some tantalizing details in the beginning that had all the hallmarks of a pattern, little more was revealed about that, which ultimately forced the students to consider that Jacqueline Woodson had something else in mind. There was something else that might explain what was going on that she wanted them to see, and so they had to lean in close again and attend to what she had to say.

In this way, we have to maintain flexibility throughout the entire text, until we reach the very end, where something slightly different happens. When we begin a book we have no idea what direction the story will take, and so we must read with an open mind, willing to entertain almost any possibility as we question and consider what the details might be showing us while not setting our thinking in stone. Endings, however, are in a sense irrevocable. This person died and that person didn't; this one won and that one lost. One by one, the doors the writers opened in the beginning have been closed, until only one or a few are left. And rather than being open and alert to all the directions the text might take as the story unfolds, readers finally reaching the end must contend with the unalterable fact that this happened and that didn't—and this requires flexibility, too, of a slightly different sort.

WE WRESTLE AND RECKON WITH THE END TO REVISE
OUR UNDERSTANDINGS ONE MORE TIME

In a sense, the end is the writer's last words in the conversation he's been having with the reader. And while, as readers, we get the final say, as we'll explore in depth in the next chapter, we want to spend time thinking about the end because in deliberately choosing to end here and not there, writers often reveal to us their preoccupations and concerns. We can see this most clearly in fairy tales and fables, where the end of the story hammers home some edifying moral or message that the writer wants us to learn: that greed and vanity cause heartbreak and grief, that hard work and humility will be rewarded. Most contemporary narratives, however, such as *Pictures of Hollis Woods* and *Because of Winn-Dixie*, aren't driven toward a single instructional message in the same way those more streamlined tales are. They are more descriptive than prescriptive, more layered and nuanced and open-ended, which leaves more room and places for readers to find their way into those deeper layers and more room for multiple interpretations to emerge from what individual readers have noticed.

But in a sense these writers are still showing us at the end that all *this* leads to *that*: that the details and patterns they've laid in the text that we've been connecting and tracking lead to a particular end that they want us to contemplate. And while we're no longer alert to "what's going to happen next"—whether that's expressed through a prediction, a wonder, a hunch, or a maybe statement—we now have to wrestle with the maybes of that end and revisit all that's led up to it in order to revise our understanding one more time. And in that reckoning we must accommodate ourselves to the text—to the fact that *this* happened, not *that*—or else, as we quoted Robert Probst earlier, we are fantasizing, not reading.

This is part of what seems to have happened to Carly, the student who had read *William's Doll*. Given the number of pages Charlotte Zolotow devoted to William rhapsodizing and begging for a doll, it seems well within the realm of possibility that a fourth-grade student might develop a hunch about him not getting it because he'd whined. But the unalterable fact of the ending is that William got what he wanted, which should have compelled her, as a reader, to reconsider what she had read and revise whatever meaning she was making of the story in light of that final development. And this process of wrestling with the end might have ultimately led her to conceive of something she had, perhaps, never thought about before—perhaps that some people wrongly pigeonhole others based on gender stereotypes, or, put more simply, that there are many different ways of being a boy or a girl.

Carly's inability to see that might also have been compounded by the particular prompt she was given. Thinking about what the main character learned can sometimes be a useful way of pointing us to the heart of a text. But in *William's Doll*, it is actually William's father, not William, who seems to have learned a lesson. And without the kind of reading process that would have engaged her in drafting and revising *as* she read, fitting and connecting pieces together, while considering what they might mean, she didn't have much to draw on. And left to her own devices, she seemingly plucked an answer out of the air, not the text. She imposed an outcome on the story, despite what the story said, rather than seeing how all the parts of a text can come together to yield a particular outcome, which carries a particular meaning.

WE KNOW THERE IS NOT A SINGLE WAY TO BUILD A FINAL UNDERSTANDING

Because texts are so varied, so complex, and sometimes even ambiguous, we know, as readers, that there is no single way of thinking that will work with every reader with every book every time. Considering what a character learned works sometimes, as does looking through the lens of problem and solution, along with what appears to be a new crop of strategies, such as "Lesson from the Elder," which asks students to look for scenes in a text where the main character is given some kind of advice by an older, wiser one, or "Tough Questions," which tells students to be on the lookout for lines where the main character asks himself a tough question, such as "Am I brave enough . . . ?" Carly might have been helped if she knew how to push into the problem-and-solution lens by asking why and how questions, which might have allowed her to provide a piece missing from the scaffold of the chart: that our *somebody*, William, *wanted* a doll, *but* his father didn't buy one for him, *so* his grandmother did, *because* she appreciated the nurturing impulse that was behind his desire. But even that alone might not have helped her had she not also been constructing her understanding of the text as she made her way attentively through it, noticing details and actively trying to fit the pieces together.

The additional problem with these strategies and prompts is that they each send students off on a kind of scavenger hunt, isolating and plucking out single lines of text, while almost begging them to ignore everything else. They may help students identify a one-word theme or answer a question on a test, but they don't help them see how readers actually construct meaning in a way that ultimately allows them to independently, through their own mental locomotion, arrive at understanding and insight. We also think it's important to note that they won't always help students meet the Common Core State Standards, which the majority of states have adopted. Unlike some previous standards, the CCSS emphasize that students link "messages, lessons, and morals" (in grade 3) or "themes" (in grades 4 and above) to details, in a way that asks them to see inductively how a theme is "determined by," "conveyed through," and "developed" by details over the course of a text.

WE TRUST TEXTS, THE PROCESS, AND OUR OWN READING RESPONSES TO REVISE OUR UNDERSTANDING

What seems more reliable—and far more authentic—than strategies and prompts that too often ask students to zoom in and extract a single meaning from a text rather than to experience and engage with it deeply is simply to trust the meaning-making process and the way that texts operate. Many of the students we saw in the last chapter who were actively constructing understandings from what they noticed as they drafted and revised their way through *Pictures of Hollis Woods* were already circling ideas that were leading them deeper into the text in a way that would ultimately yield themes. They were contemplating what the character might be learning—e.g., "Will Hollis learn how to make her own decisions and not depend so much on others?"—and thinking about how Hollis' problems might be solved—"Maybe Hollis will move on from Steven and accept her new life with Josie"—without explicitly being asked to. And for those students whose maybe statements stayed on the level of predictions about what might happen next (e.g., "Maybe Steven died" versus "Maybe Hollis trusts herself more and doesn't need an outside voice"), the fact that the book ends means that readers must deal with why and how what happened actually happened, not what's going to happen. And that's often revealed, or shown, by the final development and convergence of those patterns that the writer has pulled through to the end.

In this way, we could say, that the end of a text naturally pushes us beyond the literal level into the realm of deeper understanding. It begs readers to consider the kind of why questions we explore below. Readers also use their own authentic responses as a kind of on-ramp to think more deeply about both the end and the text as a whole. Were they pleased or sad, annoyed or relieved, or any combination thereof? In the lesson that follows, for instance, you'll also see two students struggling to accept the outcome of a story, which runs completely counter to what they'd predicted right up to the last page, by using the occasion and their reaction to the end to stretch themselves beyond what they'd previously thought in a way that allows them to grow and develop new ideas and insight, which we believe is the real goal of reading.

WE INFER TO ZOOM OUT FROM THE PARTICULARS OF THE TEXT TO THE UNIVERSAL

Finally, as we began to explore in Chapter 5, we know as readers that the particulars of a story speak to universal human conditions. On the surface we may have nothing in common with many of the texts we read—we may never, for example, have been bounced between foster homes or been able to draw, as Hollis Woods was—but the details provided by Patricia Reilly Giff allow us to feel and experience that almost as if we had lived it ourselves. And that experience ultimately allows us to consider whatever Hollis might have come to understand about herself and the world.

In the last chapter we examined how we do this before we finish a text, by engaging and dwelling in the details, but the process peaks when we finish a book. One of the most important gifts reading gives us is the ability to see ourselves in others and others in ourselves. As Peter Johnston points out, this is an act of social imagination (p. 85) and, we believe, is the essence of text-to-self connections—not the connections typically taught, where a reader often looks at what he or she literally has in common with a text—but connecting with a text by first temporarily suspending ourselves as we read, completely giving ourselves over to the world of the story. Only then can we truly begin to see what those particulars might be saying about universal human conditions.

This requires a kind of surrendering to the story, though it's far from a passive act. Making this move from the particulars to the universal—or, as we frequently say to students, zooming out from the book into the world—requires one last act of inferring. The good news is that when we've been engaged and invested in tracking patterns and have wrestled with the end, this move is often not so hard to make. Many students, in fact, do it quite naturally, moving fluidly from the particulars to the universal, as did the fifth grader who, while reading *Pictures of Hollis Woods*, connected the pattern about Josie needing Hollis to Hollis never having felt needed before and said, "Maybe Josie is [Hollis'] family now; feeling needed is family love." And others who don't do this quite so automatically get the hang of it pretty quickly when the moves are explicitly noticed and named.

As readers, we make this move much as we did in Chapter 5, by positing answers to questions that often remain invisible in our minds. What's different here are the questions that the end finally asks us to consider: Why did the author do this and not that? Why did she end it this way? What might that say about the story as a whole? What is it *really* about?

We can't, of course, answer these questions for others since each reader's answer is an outgrowth of the conversation they've had with the author. And so what matters, finally, is that each reader does the work. Readers do not read words and then wait for someone else to tell us what they mean, nor do they read words and then identify the literary elements. We read words and build living and breathing ideas from them—ideas that matter to us and continue to develop as we talk with each other, keep reading, and talk some more. When readers actively make meaning from what they notice, we become more deeply invested and engaged in the texts we read, which, in turn, helps us notice more deeply, which further deepens our understanding.

If we allow students to do this, we are confident not only that they will be able to answer multiple-choice questions about theme on tests and write essays that contain thematic statements but also that they will be motivated to pick up another book and another, actively participating in the conversation that is understanding. And so in this lesson, we aim to help students experience the following:

* Make final revisions of their understandings of a text as they reach the end

* Take into account how parts of the text come together at the end

* Use their reactions to a text as a means to revise and think deeper

* Zoom out from the particulars of a text to see something more universal

* Develop agency by constructing their own understandings

What This Looks Like in Classrooms

We are in another fourth-grade room, this time in Harlem, using the book *A Taste of Blackberries* by Doris Buchanan Smith (1973) to help students see and actually experience the process of meaning making. *A Taste of Blackberries* is an odd little book, told by a first-person narrator whose name we never find out. It begins with a handful of scenes that show us a seemingly imperfect friendship between two boys, with the narrator becoming increasingly irritated by his friend, Jamie, who he thinks is a joker and a show-off. But then the book takes an unexpected turn: Jamie dies from an allergic reaction to a bee sting. The narrator is at first convinced that Jamie is faking his reaction to the sting in order to get attention, and many of the students in the class also haven't been convinced that Jamie is actually dead. In fact, the question "Is Jamie really dead?" has stayed in the WONDER column of our ever-useful chart as we have made our way through the rest of the book.

As we introduced the notion of patterns, described in Chapter 5, the students began to notice that the narrator keeps describing moments with Jamie as if he were still alive. Different students have interpreted this pattern in different ways, however. One group has constructed a maybe statement that the narrator might be pretending or wishing that Jamie was still alive, while the other group, often using the very same details, as you can see in Figure 6.1, has thought that Jamie might not, in fact, be dead and might come back in some way—perhaps even through an act of magic, which they think is possible because of a line each group noted on their chart but interpreted differently: "The soap was my lamp and I was Aladdin. I would rub life back for Jamie."

Now, though, we have reached the last page without Jamie materializing. The narrator has just brought a basket of blackberries to Jamie's mother and talked to her for the first time since her son's death. And after having been warmly received by her, he is now running out to play, which leads us to the very last lines:

> In my relief I felt that Jamie, too, was glad the main sadness was over. I wondered how fast angels, or whatever he was now, could move.
> "Race you," I called to him, and I ran up the hill. (p. 85)

Pattern We Notice: "I" is *always* thinking about Jamie as if he were still alive.	
What This Makes Us Wonder: Is Jamie Really Dead?	
The narrator's mother tells him Jamie is dead (p. 33).	"I didn't want to listen to her telling me lies about Jamie" (p. 34).
He's remembering times when they used to play together. "No more blinks from across the street at night. No more Jamie" (p. 39).	They're playing with each other, doing Morse code with tin cans and string (p. 37).
"Dad and Mom were getting ready to go to the funeral parlor. They asked me if I wanted to go, but I couldn't do that to Jamie. It seemed that as long as I acted like he wasn't dead, he wouldn't be dead" (p. 40).	"They asked me if I wanted to go, but I couldn't do that to Jamie. It seemed that as long as I acted like he wasn't dead, he wouldn't be dead" (p. 40).
"I thought of me and Jamie throwing stones in a still pond, watching ripples. Jamie wouldn't make ripples anymore. Or shampoo beards. I grabbed the soap and rubbed up a lather. The soap was my lamp and I was Aladdin. I would rub life back for Jamie" (p. 41).	"I thought of me and Jamie throwing stones in a still pond, watching ripples. Jamie wouldn't make ripples anymore. Or shampoo beards. I grabbed the soap and rubbed up a lather. The soap was my lamp and I was Aladdin. I would rub life back for Jamie" (p. 41).
"It began to sink in that Jamie wasn't going to open his eyes to stare back at me. He wasn't going to blink. He wasn't going to laugh" (p. 45).	"It just didn't seem possible that a tiny thing like a bee could kill you" (p. 42).
	". . . if it was possible that Jamie knew what was going on, I wanted him to know that I was here, thinking about him" (p. 44).

(continues)

(continued)

The narrator couldn't see the beam because Jamie isn't there to play with his flashlight because he's dead (p. 46).	"I flicked on my light and shined it over toward Jamie's to see if I could see his flashlight. Of course I couldn't. The beam didn't carry that far" (p. 46).
The narrator cries and cries at the end of Chapter 5 because he finally realizes Jamie is dead.	He still calls it Jamie's house.
Maybe Statement: Maybe the narrator wishes that Jamie was alive.	**Maybe Statement:** Maybe Jamie isn't really dead and will come back.

Figure 6–1. Chart of students tracking a pattern that leads them to develop two different maybe statements

We read the lines, then ceremoniously close the book, prepared to start talking about a reader's job at the end of the book. But Jose, one of the students who has held out for Jamie to reappear, blurts out in frustration, "What kind of a book has the main character die in the beginning?"

We can practically feel him mentally hurling the book across the room. This is not at all what we intended—that our instruction would reinforce the belief that there are right and wrong answers in books and the "good" readers get those answers right while "bad" readers get them wrong. Jose and many of the others who believed that Jamie hadn't really died were, up till now, students who hadn't always felt confident or successful as readers. Several of them had interpreted the patterns they had tracked as pointing to an external event—i.e., a miraculous recovery or Jamie returning as a zombie—not an internal development in the narrator's feelings or thinking. We know that, for them, this moment is key, and that we must teach them how readers construct meaning from whatever they have noticed and experienced with a text or perhaps risk them feeling even more unsuccessful. And we also must ensure that the rest of the class doesn't see the process of reading as leading to a right or a wrong.

What we do as teachers:
We seize student responses as teaching opportunities.

So we take a deep breath and plunge into the fracas, seizing what's just happened as a teaching opportunity, something to value and appreciate, not to dismiss or ignore.

"I think that what some of us are experiencing now is connected to how challenging endings can be. All throughout the book we've kept our minds open, using that great thinking word 'maybe,' knowing that the patterns we noticed were taking us somewhere, but not being really sure where. But when we reach the end, there are no more maybes—at least not in terms of what's going to happen. And so we have to deal with the fact that all those patterns were leading us to this place, not that place. And for some of us that means accepting that what we'd thought or hoped might happen didn't."

We explain to the students then that it's not a question of right or wrong. Instead it's a question of revision, bringing the point home by reminding them of what they all had to do in the beginning, when everyone thought that, being a show-off and a risk-taker, Jamie was going to do something to get the narrator into trouble. Many had hunches about what the narrator might do if that did happen, with a few even thinking about how that might impact their friendship in a larger way. But when Jamie was stung by the bee, the whole class had to regroup and revise, wrapping their minds around this sudden turn that the writer wanted us to make for some purpose we had yet to discern.

In this way, we use the students' own experience as the model for what must be done now, knowing that their previous success with revising will help them do what is for many children—and many adults, as well—a difficult move to make. For just when we think we don't have to think anymore, we have to rethink yet again. We anticipate that it might be especially challenging for students like Jose, whose comment suggests he's at risk for checking out because he feels that he's been toyed with by the writer and has ended up at the "losing" side of what had all the makings of dueling interpretations. Once again, it feels like a critical moment, with a reader's investment and engagement at stake. And so we want to assure Jose and many of his classmates that their reaction to the book is well within the realm of a reasonable reader's response, while still nudging them to consider and think about what this ending means in terms of the author's possible intention. And so we push into Jose's question as the means to get the whole class thinking, while offering him what constitutes a reader's right of refusal:

"Here again, the writer's taken us to a place that isn't what some of us expected and we have to revise our thinking. This doesn't mean we have to like where we are. In fact, there are lots of times that readers decide they don't like a book because of the ending or because they feel the writer's let them down. But before we make that final call, I think we all need to consider Jose's question: 'What kind of a book has the main character die in the beginning?' It's actually a question every reader needs to ask, even if a book turns out the way you had expected: Why did the writer do what she did? What might she be wanting us to think about by telling the story the way that she did and then ending it this way?"

What we do as teachers: *We invite students to think about the author's purpose in deep, text-specific ways.*

We write Jose's question on our KNOW/WONDER chart, then explain that we want everyone to try to draft one more maybe statement, because despite the fact that we've reached the end there are still questions and maybes to explore—not maybes about what will happen, but about what that might mean. Then we ask the students to once again turn and talk, positioning some of the charts about the patterns the students have noticed and the maybe statement that grew out of them next to the interactive white board where we project the last page of the book to keep them grounded in the text. Then we make a point of going to listen to Jose and his partner, David, talk.

"Well," Jose begins slowly, looking at the words on the screen, "that last line. It's like Jamie's still alive and he's talking to him, just like those other times."

"Yeah," says David.

"But now," Jose states firmly, "I think it's in his head."

"Yeah, his imagination," agrees David.

"Wow," we respond. "That's a big change from what you thought before. You both really revised your thinking! What made you do that?"

"It says he's an angel," David says, pointing at the words on the screen.

"Yeah, it's like he's there but not there," Jose adds on.

"Can you say more about why you think that?" we ask.

"Well," Jose says, glancing at the pattern charts, "they're still friends but when he [the narrator] is talking to Jamie it's in his mind."

"That's why we were so confused," David says. "Because it was his imagination."

At this point both boys grow silent, and so we make the decision to jump in, trying to carefully walk that fine line between a scaffold and a prompt in order to validate their experience and reactions as readers and invite them to keep thinking. "Do you think it's possible that the author was confusing you on purpose, that she *wanted* her readers to think that Jamie might come back?"

What we do as teachers: *We honor students' experiences with texts in a way that empowers them as readers.*

"Maybe," Jose says.

"We know what a great thinking word 'maybe' is, so let's keep thinking about this for a minute. If she did do that on purpose, why might she have done that? Why would an author confuse a reader and make you think that a character might not really be dead?"

David answered without hesitation. "I think the author's saying that people aren't so easy to forget. When they die they don't come back. You want them to but they don't."

Jose nods. "He [the narrator] didn't want Jamie to be dead. He kept hoping." Then he paused a moment and said, "Losing someone is really, really hard."

We don't know what personal experience Jose may or may not have had with the loss of a loved one, but we have seen the thinking journey he has been on as a reader, and so our hearts flood with empathy and pride. In the course of perhaps ten minutes he has gone from dismissing a book to really reading it. We want to celebrate and name this for the benefit of the rest of the class, so we reconvene the class and share what Jose and David have recognized, naming the moves they made to get where they finally did:

We explain how they began by looking at the very last line, where the narrator says, "Race you" to Jamie, and realized that the line was connected to the pattern they'd already noticed—all those details that sounded like Jamie wasn't really dead. But this time, because they were here, at the very end, when nothing else was going to happen, they realized that they had to make sense of the lines they'd just read. So they looked really hard at that last line about Jamie being an angel and thought about all those other times they'd noticed the author being purposely confusing. Putting all that together, they revised their original idea about Jamie not being dead and decided that it was the narrator talking to him in his head.

"This made them think," we say, "that the author may have told the story this way, with all those purposefully confusing details, because she wanted us to know that even though Jamie was dead, their friendship still lived on."

We pause here, letting our words sink in but knowing that we also want to make visible for everyone the move that Jose and David made from the particulars of the story to the universals.

"But Jose and David didn't stop their thinking there," we say. "As they jumped into the story and tried to make sense of everything the writer put into it—including some of those confusing patterns—they realized something else. They realized that the book was not just about these characters but about people in general—that through the story of this friendship the writer was exploring something about all our lives, which is how very, very hard it is to lose someone and how badly we want them to come back. In fact, sometimes we want them to come back so badly we can't believe they're really gone.

What we do as teachers: *We notice and name what students do to make the process of meaning making transferable to other texts.*

"When readers do this, it really helps us connect to books—to understand something about the characters, about life, and about why people do the things they do, which is at the heart of why we read to begin with."

We then invite the other students to share out their thinking, noticing and naming the work they've done, too, and supporting students, when necessary, as they move from the particulars of the story to the more universal ideas or themes, as Jose and David have masterfully done. We hear many students echo some of Jose and David's thinking in different words: Some talk about holding onto memories for comfort; some talk about the guilt they noticed the narrator felt about being alive and how "bad" feelings can stay with you; some dwell in the scene at the end when the narrator's interaction with Jamie's mother leaves him smiling, and talk about how, no matter how bad you feel, some things will always make you feel better.

To help them hold onto what they did and replicate it with other texts, we end the session by co-constructing a chart (Figure 6–2) that names the various kinds of thinking different students engaged in. And we send the students back to their desks, promising that we'll return the next day to complete the meaning-making cycle by thinking about what the book might have to say to us in our own lives.

Digging Deeper into Books
Strategies We Use to Consider What an Author Might Be Exploring
▶ Revise our hunches and maybe statements as we find new information–especially at the end.   ▶ Try to make sense of the patterns we notice throughout the text.   ▶ Talk with each other to make sense of confusing parts.   ▶ Think about what the author might be trying to show us about people and life.   ▶ Zoom out from the story into the world.

Figure 6–2. Co-created anchor chart on how to continue building and revising understandings of the themes beneath the surface of a text

What We Do as Teachers

WE NOTICE AND NAME WHAT STUDENTS DO TO MAKE THE PROCESS OF MEANING MAKING TRANSFERABLE TO OTHER TEXTS AND OTHER STUDENTS

The ability to transfer and apply skills and knowledge from one setting to another is one of the hallmarks of student independence and higher-level thinking. With these goals in mind, we design our instruction to make abstract thinking visible so that students are better able to do what they've done with one text to another, including those of increasing difficulty. Thus, we teach the reader, not the reading of any given text, and the process over the product. This means, ver, too, that we, too, have to move from the particulars of whatever a student is saying about a text or a character to the more general work he is doing, which requires practice on our end, as well.

Here, for instance, we noticed, named, and charted the moves that Jose and David made to grow and construct their ideas so as to make them more replicable. We also noticed and named the different sequence and combinations of moves that other students used to arrive at their understandings in order to emphasize that there is no single way or step-by-step procedure that works for every student with every text. Some wrestled first with the particulars—the narrator talking to Jamie's mother, his smile, his words to Jamie at the end—fitting and connecting those final details with the patterns they'd already noticed and revising when necessary before they zoomed out to the universal. Others leapt straight to universals, then went back to the particulars to name what made them think that; while still others began by focusing on what the ending made them feel and zoomed both in and out from there, going back to the text and out into the world.

The chart thus acts as a reminder of everything all the students did to make meaning. But beyond this support, we believe that the students in this room—in particular Jose and David—will carry this experience of meaning making with them in a way that will make their excursions into new books qualitatively different. They have not just seen or listened to but have experienced how a reader can plunge into the world of the text, with all its specificity, its uniqueness, and its quirks, and emerge pages later with an understanding about human nature and life that extends way beyond the book's cover. And we believe that from the start of their next book they will know to expect significance because they have seen how it is woven into all aspects of a text, deliberately seeking meaning because they now know it is there, invisible but accessible if they attend to what they notice and let those noticings lead them to notice more.

WE SEIZE STUDENT RESPONSES AS TEACHING OPPORTUNITIES

We began this book by looking at what research has suggested are the two prime ingredients of effective teaching: the particular kind of content knowledge that, when it comes to reading, understands how students actually make meaning along with all the various ways they can misunderstand or get stuck, and the ability to interactively respond to offer emotional, social, and instructional support. As we noted in the last chapter, however, this presents some planning challenges. We have a road map that lets us know the main outline of the trip, which we articulate for ourselves. But we also must articulate all those ways that students can get derailed so as to be better able to support them, both emotionally and instructionally, when they get bogged down.

Here, for instance, we know that real reading—reading that actually allows us to construct our own individualized meaning, rather than assume someone else's—requires a flexible, open mind that is willing to readjust and even discard thinking, to share fledgling thoughts before they're fully formed, and to tolerate a fair amount of uncertainty. Many students struggle with this, in good part, we fear, because too much of what happens in schools—and all that happens on tests—values answers over questions and certitude over receptivity. Knowing this, we not only attempt to facilitate those experiences that will push students beyond right-or-wrong thinking, but we seize the moments when that kind of thinking pokes up its head, as it often does around predictions, to remind students, as we do here, that being right matters less to readers than being open and flexible, as evinced through the act of revising.

We also know that many students are literal thinkers who struggle to get past the event-level of plot, which predictions encourage them to stick to, to see the deeper, less visible layers. And so when the conversation turns on whose maybe statement was right, we close that door by opening another, asking them, now that the plot has ended at this particular point, to consider not what might happen next, but what this final turn of events might mean. Freed from speculating about what happens, most of the literal-minded students in the room are able to use the final reckoning opportunity that endings provide to catapult themselves into those deeper levels where the heart of meaning lies. For those who still aren't yet able to do so, Jose and David's story becomes a powerful model and incentive that, with repeated opportunities to practice, we know they'll eventually replicate.

Finally, we seize on Jose's statement of frustration, seeing in it the germ of a question we know all readers must ask: "What is this book really about?" We'll unpack below what we see as being gained by bringing that question forward, but here we pause to notice and name it as another instance in which we combine our knowledge of the process and our awareness of the challenges students face with the need to respond interactively on the social, emotional, and instructional levels.

Of course, this combination can be difficult to plan for, since we must be open and flexible, too, ready to revise and reconsider our instruction in a way prepackaged lesson plans or curricula simply do not allow for. And so we engage in a process of planning that educators Matt Glover and Mary Alice Berry (2011) have dubbed "I Can't Know But I Can Project." We determine our essential goals by articulating for ourselves the thinking work involved in the process of meaning making we want to guide our students through, then use that to project a rough sequence of lessons that will allow students to experience the different parts and thinking involved in that process. We also consider the supports they might need, knowing where the pitfalls and stumbling blocks are. But we make the final determination about what to teach when based on what we notice students doing with our instruction, each other, and the text. Thus, as Glover and Berry state, "we are ensuring that we are prepared to respond thoughtfully to the numerous opportunities to make decisions that comprise the world of teaching" (p. 19)—ready to seize those teaching moments when they fall into our hands.

WE HONOR STUDENTS' EXPERIENCES WITH TEXTS IN A WAY THAT EMPOWERS THEM AS READERS

When we move from teaching texts to teaching readers, one of the main challenges we face as teachers is letting what we may perceive as misreadings stand uncorrected. In this instance, we're aware, as readers, that Jamie has, indeed, died and that Jose and David and the other students who interpreted the details they collected as suggesting that he wasn't really dead could be seen as an example of readers who are not accommodating themselves to the text—who are fantasizing, not reading. We're also aware that we could have stepped in at any number of points to "correct" their miscomprehension by drawing their attention to other details that clearly point to Jamie being gone. That might, in fact, have spared them the frustration and embarrassment Jose, in particular, seemed to feel when, on reaching the end, his prediction turned out not to have come true. But prompting them to revise their thinking before they were actually ready risked confirming their already established belief that meaning in a book resided outside their capabilities, interest, or stamina. And it would have short-circuited the process of meaning making for both of them, which would have further imperiled both their sense of identity and agency—and their willingness to engage with whatever they read next.

Additionally, we're aware that our ability to grasp that Jamie did, indeed, die is connected to our experience with both life and texts. Developmentally, we know that some fourth graders still practice the kind of magical thinking that led some to believe that it might be possible for the narrator to rub soap like a genie's lamp and bring Jamie back to life. Also, many of the students had never encountered a book where a child died before, nor experienced it in their lives, which made that outcome seem beyond the realm of possibilities to them. And so, just as we did with the miscomprehensions that resulted from missed textual clues in Chapter 3, we let any thinking that has been constructed from patterns and details stand, trusting that texts and the process of meaning making will help students accommodate themselves and not simply fantasize.

Finally, we believe that a reader's understanding of a text grows not only from the details and patterns they notice and the meaning they make of those, but of what they experience emotionally as they read. Jose and David, for instance, clung to the belief that Jamie hadn't died, in much the way the narrator himself did. And when they had to acknowledge that he had died, they were crushed, not simply because they'd failed to comprehend that but perhaps also because they felt the weight of the loss and a sense of anger and betrayal at a world in which such things could happen.

These powerful emotions were, in effect, authentic reader responses that grew out of their engagement with the text, not from a prompt or assignment. We'll talk more in the next chapter about how readers use their gut responses to evaluate a text, along with how the kinds of written responses we often ask students to complete miss the mark. But here we note that honoring those responses allowed the two boys to not only "see" but to feel what the author seemed to be saying in a way that gave their revised understanding more depth and resonance than any single word, like *death* or *grief* or *guilt*, might have had.

We did, though, of course, have to nudge them a bit in a way that always makes us redefine for ourselves that line between a prompt and a scaffold. Here, we try to stay on the scaffolding side of that line by talking about readers and writers, with the particulars of the text only used to help them consider how a reader's response might inform whatever meaning a reader makes of what the writer has provided, without sanctioning or pushing them toward a specific meaning, which we believe is almost always a prompt's secret agenda. We also consider what our intervention accomplished. On the one hand it helped Jose and David move from the literal—i.e., Jamie died—to the more thematic— "Losing someone is really hard"—while preserving full ownership of the meaning they made. And it ultimately allowed them to feel successful as readers. But it also had other benefits, for as Maxine Greene (1988) writes, "Children who have been provoked to reach beyond themselves, to wonder, to imagine, to pose their own questions are the ones mostly likely to learn to learn" (p. 14). By allowing them to pose their own question, even when it erupted out of anger, and then giving them space to ponder the answer, they reached beyond what they already knew to arrive at a new level of insight, which increased not only their openness to reading but their potential to learn.

> **Rethinking our practice:**
> *We use authentic readers' responses as a tool to dig deeper into a text, not as an assignment to assess comprehension.*

WE CHOOSE THE LANGUAGE WE USE TO TEACH LITERARY ELEMENTS CAREFULLY, INTRODUCING ACADEMIC TERMS ONLY ONCE STUDENTS HAVE EXPERIENCED THEM

As much as we believe in the importance of academic terminology, we fear that this terminology is meaningless if students don't first experience it. And so, just as we did with strategies in Chapter 4, we try to talk about literary elements in an accessible and kid-friendly way, waiting to introduce more academic language until students have some actual experience to attach those terms to and a better understanding of what they authentically mean and can do for a reader.

Thus in this lesson, we don't use the word *theme*, though theme is clearly what this class of fourth-grade students have arrived at through the process of making meaning. Having experienced that process deeply, however, we feel confident that if we introduce the term at this point they will have no problem understanding what it means, as many lower and middle school students do. The sad fact is that when we ask students what the word *theme* means, we too often hear them talk about it in terms of a decoration focus, as in a party that has a vampire or a Wild West theme. We suppose those could be considered "unifying ideas," which is how theme is sometimes defined in reference books, but they seem to miss the point. And we have to assume they miss it in part because we have failed to give them a sense of what the word really means, or opportunities to experience for themselves how a theme is organically grown and developed from our thoughtful engagement with a text.

We also believe that the problem is compounded by the kind of scavenger hunt prompts we discussed earlier and the reductive, fill-in-the-blank approach to theme found in many workbooks and online resources. We can download lesson plans, including reproducibles, on defining theme, identifying theme, and choosing the right theme out of a lineup of multiple-choice answers. But of all the skills involved in reading, considering what the writer might be trying to show us about what it means to be human through the particulars of a story as they're conveyed through details is surely the most important—and the most difficult.

Rethinking our practice: *We never ask students to identify a theme; rather we help students construct an understanding out of which theme can emerge.*

Disconnecting that from the actual experience of making one's way through a text, accumulating and revising understanding as you go, as so many of the online lesson plans do, shortchanges the heart and soul of reading and thinking. We are therefore careful with labels and always "name" academic terms after students first have a chance to experience and notice.

Similarly, we didn't explicitly teach or discuss problem and solution to either this class or the fifth graders reading *Pictures of Hollis Woods* in the last chapter. Nor did we ask students to consider what they think a character learned. Had we done so here we think it quite possible that Jose and David might have said something like "The narrator learned not to stick your hand in a beehive," which is, indeed, something the narrator learned, but like the answer given by our *William's Doll* student, Carly, it misses the mark.

As happens in downloadable theme lessons, much of the teaching we see around problem and solution seems to end at identification, and as such, is divorced from the process of making meaning. This is especially true when instruction focuses on categorizing problems by identifying them as internal conflicts or conflicts with another person, society, nature, and, in some lists, machine. We can certainly teach students to do this, and many of them do it well, but it does little to help them think deeply about a text or consider what it opened their hearts or minds to. Instead, if we focus on students connecting and tracking whatever patterns they notice while they continue to draft and revise and reckon with the outcome of the story at the end, we see students naturally thinking about what a character learned or how they solved their problem without us prompting them to do so—just as we saw why questions emerge as students considered the significance of details and began to notice patterns without us directly teaching them to question.

For all these reasons, we never end our teaching of literary elements at identification, but push deeper into them so that students can see and actually experience how, as writer Jayne Anne Phillips (2009) says, "Fiction is the slow apprehension of meaning through the elements of story and language" (p. 11). We don't read to find literary elements; we use literary elements to read.

> **Rethinking our practice:**
> *Rather than teaching students to identify literary elements, we help them see how writers and readers use those elements to apprehend meaning.*

WE INVITE STUDENTS TO THINK ABOUT THE AUTHOR'S PURPOSE IN DEEP, TEXT-SPECIFIC WAYS

As we did on the heels of reading "Food. Music. Memory.," we note here how inadequate the words we find in classrooms to express an author's purpose—i.e., *inform*, *persuade*, and *entertain*—actually are when we've really thought about and engaged with a text. Surely Doris Buchanan Smith didn't write *A Taste of Blackberries* to entertain us, nor does she seem to be trying to persuade us. We could say she is trying to inform us of all the complicated, conflicting emotions we go through when someone we care about dies, though she does so in a way that's far more indirect than your typical fact-filled information text.

This is, we fear, another example of reductive thinking that actually does little to help students make meaning. And so we reframe the whole notion of author's purpose, beginning by helping students see over time that texts have been carefully orchestrated, with every word, every detail, there for a reason that we can't discern at first but will if we read carefully and thoughtfully with the question "why" on our shoulders: Why is the author showing me this? Why do these details keep repeating? Why are the characters doing what they're doing? Why is the story told this way?

Of course, sometimes when we ask these questions without providing additional scaffolds such as we did in Chapter 5, we get generic responses such as these: "Because it's more interesting that way" or "We won't know unless we ask the author." Students frequently need to experience how all the pieces of a text come together to reveal something lasting and meaningful—or to feel a greater sense of agency, like the three students in Chapter 5, who just wanted to be told what to do—before they are able to carry those why questions. But, as we'll see below in the conference with a student who has been through the process before, once you have "seen" meaning in one book, you know to ask "What could this mean?" in other books. Once you've experienced the "aha"

Rethinking our practice:
We frame the idea of author's purpose around a text's meaning, not generic terms like inform, entertain, *or* persuade.

of insight, seeing how a pattern yields understanding, how the pieces all dovetail together, you're prone to more purposefully look for it again, until you eventually develop the habit, as lifelong readers have, of moving from word to meaning as automatically as readers move from the letters *c, a, t* to the word *cat.*

Making Every Student's Thinking Visible

ASSESSING A STUDENT'S ABILITY TO TRANSFER AND APPLY SKILLS TO AN INDEPENDENT READING BOOK

As you've seen before, we use small groups to offer students additional time and support to practice one particular aspect of the complicated work of reading with a text or an excerpt we've chosen for that purpose. With conferences our aim is different. We use the opportunity conferring gives us to see what students are doing and making with the words they're encountering in a book of their choosing in a way that often allows us to assess what they are—or aren't—taking away from the read-aloud.

Here we confer with Ahmed, one of the seventh graders who had participated in the meaning-making process with *Miracle's Boys,* to see how he was—or wasn't—transferring that experience to another text. We find him a little more than halfway through *Game*, a novel by Walter Dean Myers (2008) that we've never read, which always presents challenges for us as teachers. In fact, many teachers we work with express doubt about how they can confer with students in smart ways in a book they themselves haven't read. But before we ask him to open the book and read a little to us, we want to get a feel for what, if anything, he may be doing differently as a reader on the heels of *Miracle's Boys*. And so we ask the following question, which positions students to talk about themselves as readers, rather than about the content of the book:

"So, Ahmed, is there anything you think you're trying to do as a reader with this book?"

"Well," he says thoughtfully, "I think I'm reading slower than I used to. Like in the beginning, it was really confusing, but I tried to slow down so I could figure stuff out and that worked pretty well. And now I guess I'm sort of looking for those 'always' things and I'm noticing more."

"That's great," we say, curbing the impulse to ask him for examples, because the fact of the matter is that having not read the book ourselves, we simply won't be able to assess whether he's really comprehended what he's read or not, let alone embarked on the harder work of drafting an understanding from what he's noticed. We know our time will be better spent by seeing what his mind does with new words on a page that we can look at as well. And so instead we ask Ahmed to open the book and begin reading where he left off, and he quickly turns to page 140, scans the page to find his place, then reads the following:

> *A skinny dude with crack-shiny eyes stopped us, let us glimpse a watch, and shoved it back into his pocket. "You need a Rolex?" he asked, looking around. "Fifty dollars."*
>
> *"Where am I going to get fifty dollars?" Ruffy asked.*
>
> *"Ten dollars because you look like a right-on brother," Shiny Eyes said.*
>
> *"I ain't got it, my man." Ruffy held his hands up as we walked by. . . .*

"So what you think about Tomas?" I asked as we crossed the street.

"He might have to get his butt kicked to realize this is our hood and not his," Ruffy said. "When people get stuff handed to them too easy, they think they deserved it."

I hadn't thought of it that way. Tomas probably figured he was just supposed to get to Baldwin and take over the team.

I got home and Jocelyn was standing on a chair in the kitchen running her mouth. Mom signaled for me to sit down. I didn't want to, but I did want to hear what Jocelyn was up on the chair for.

". . . So, my loyal subjects, I have had to make a difficult and painful decision. Now many of you might wonder why a perfect person like me has to make hard decisions. . . ."

"Jocelyn, say what you have to say, please," Mom said.

"I have passed the test for Stuyvesant High School and now must decide if I am to remain at Baldwin. . . ."

I put my hands out and Jocelyn slapped me five. Stuyvesant was big-time to math and science nuts, and Jocelyn had wanted to go there ever since she was in fifth grade, so I knew what "painful" answer she was going to come up with.

Mom listened to the whole speech, smiling and nodding her head. . . .

As Ahmed reads, we read over his shoulder, having learned through our years of conferring with students that because of the way texts are put together—with details that have been deliberately chosen to help "show" what the writer is exploring—we, as experienced readers, can dip into a book at almost any point and get a sense of what the writer's concerns might be on a single page, along with a feel for the kinds of demands the text puts on its readers. Here, for instance, we note that the first half of the passage presents many comprehension challenges, with a reader needing to know how dialogue works just to figure out who's talking to whom, as well as how to keep track of many characters and references like Baldwin, which we, ourselves, don't get until we reach its second appearance and infer that it's the name of a school.

The second half of the passage, while not as challenging to comprehend, does gives us a glimpse of what Walter Dean Myers might be up to. As the narrator moves from the street to his home, we sense that he seems to be straddling two worlds, one marked by hustling, drugs, and violence, and the other by family and academic aspirations. As always, it isn't our intention to get Ahmed to see what we see in the text, but being aware of what this page holds, at both the level of comprehension and understanding, we are better able to assess how deeply Ahmed is thinking. And so after we assure ourselves that he's followed the tricky first half by explaining who the characters are (including naming the narrator as Drew) and what he thinks is going on in a way that seems generally in keeping with what we surmised from the page, we ask him if what he's read right now connects with anything else he's been thinking.

"Well," he says again, gathering his thoughts. "I noticed that Jocelyn's always annoying but her mom always lets her get away with stuff, like here," he says, pointing to the place where Jocelyn is standing on the chair holding forth, in Ahmed's words, "like a princess or something."

"And, this kid here," he says, pointing to the name *Tomas*, "he's the new kid on the basketball team that the coach thinks is great—sort of like Drew's mom thinks Jocelyn is great. And Drew's worried that the coach is going let Tomas take his place sort of like he's worried about his mom because he doesn't have good grades like Jocelyn does."

"Wow," we say, "sounds like you just connected a couple of patterns. That's exactly what readers do! You're seeing something similar between what's going on between Drew, Tomas, and the coach and Drew, his sister, and his mom. Do you have any hunches about what that might mean, that Drew seems to be having the same sort of problems with his coach and Tomas and his sister and his mom?"

"Not really," Ahmed says with a shrug.

We're quite impressed with what Ahmed has done here, connecting different threads of the story together by recognizing there's a similar dynamic at play. He hasn't seen what we had seen, but the depth of his thinking makes us feel confident that the understanding work he's shared with us was built on a solid comprehension. And as a student who'd struggled before to move beyond the level of events, we are thrilled to see him carrying so much of the work of the read-aloud to this new text. And so we want to close the conference by noticing and naming the shrug he made as part of the work that readers do, too, by telling him that his "not really" might simply mean "not yet"—as in, he might not yet be ready to make a hunch without first reading further.

"And actually that's a great thing," we say, "to not jump too soon to a hunch or a maybe statement, but to keep reading forward wondering what's under these patterns you've noticed. Why does the same thing seem to be happening to Drew on the court and at home and how is he going to deal with it? And what might Walter Dean Myers be trying to show us by having all this happen to him?"

"We'll be really eager to see what you discover," we add as Ahmed nods his head. And before we can gather our notebook up to move on to the next student, Ahmed is already back in the book, picking up where he left off.

WHAT THIS LESSON ALLOWS THIS STUDENT (AND US, AS TEACHERS) TO DO

As we discussed in the last chapter after we conferred with the student reading *Identical*, conferences give us an opportunity to notice and name what students are doing in a way that supports both their identity and agency as readers. Our opening question, which specifically addresses Ahmed as a reader, supports both those aims, as well as does honoring his hesitance to posit a hunch at this point in the book. Here we also have an opportunity to assess Ahmed's ability to transfer what he's learned from the read-aloud and to support him by reminding him of the steps readers take when they start to notice patterns. Thus, just as with our *Identical* reader, the content of our conference isn't actually the text that the student is reading but the process of meaning making that, in this case, we've introduced to the class through a read-aloud. Reframing conferences around the process, not the text—and recognizing how much we can actually gather about what demands the texts puts on a student and how that student is meeting those demands—has made us confident that all of us, as teachers, can confer with students on whatever they happen to be reading, whether we've read the text ourselves or not. In fact, in this conference, Ahmed is actually the more astute reader, seeing even more in the passage than we had, which we would never have been aware of had we only been looking for *our* meaning, not his.

Rethinking How We Teach Reading	
What We Used To Do . . .	**What We Do Now . . .**
We used to teach theme as a single abstract word, such as *love*, *friendship*, *bravery*, *death*, that the text seemed mostly "about."	We now teach students to discover what an author might be saying about those single words, thinking about theme as "What *about* what it's about?"
We used to ask students to identify the theme or message of a text once they finished a text.	We now teach students that themes emerge through a conversation we have with the author that begins on the very first page.
We used to use a variety of strategies to help students access a text's theme, such as thinking about what a character learned or looking at problem and solution.	We now trust that students will construct thematic understandings if we teach them to stick close to the details and the patterns in the text, ask why questions, and draft and revise their answers.
We used to create pacing calendars for units, with specific strings of lessons, each with specific teaching points, planned for each week.	We now articulate for ourselves what we want students to understand and where we anticipate they'll need support and then project that into a rough sequence of lessons that we teach depending on where our students are.
We used to think of reading responses as prompted written assignments that we'd use to assess students' comprehension and hold them accountable for their independent reading.	We now use students' authentic responses and reactions as another way of digging deeper into a text as they consider what in the text made them react or feel the way they did.

(continues)

(continued)

We used to think of the author's purpose in terms of genre–i.e., were they trying to entertain us with a narrative, inform us through nonfiction, or persuade us through an essay?	We now think of the author's purpose as connected to whatever universals the author may be exploring through the particulars of the story.

Chapter Seven

How Readers Evaluate the Worth of a Text by Questioning and Considering Its Relevance

To read without reflecting is like eating without digesting.

—Edmund Burke

We are in a gifted and talented third-grade class whose teacher has asked us to help her address something she's worried about. Her students have been studying fables to familiarize themselves with the genre and consider an author's big ideas. And while on the one hand, things are going well, she, like many of the teachers we work with, have that nagging, troubling sense that her students could be doing more.

"Most of the kids," she explains to us, "are able to say what they think the fable's message is. But it all seems so pat, so cut-and-dried. It's like they're on an assembly line and they have a rubber stamp in their hands. And as soon as they finish reading, they stamp the story with a saying, like 'Never judge a book by a cover,' or 'Two wrongs don't make a right.' Then they're off to the next one, ready to stamp it, without ever thinking or questioning whether those ideas hold any weight."

She shows us what she means when she brings the class together to discuss a fable they've recently read. It's a retelling of the Aesop story about the wind and the sun who, during an argument about who was stronger, decided to settle the matter by seeing who can get a passing traveler to take off the coat he's wearing, with the wind trying to blow the coat off and the sun blazing down and creating such heat that the man eventually takes the coat off himself.

The teacher has the children turn to their partner to ensure that every student is thinking, and sure enough, almost to a T, every partnership comes up with a kid-friendly variation of kindness being more effective than force—or as many of the students say, "It's better to be nice than mean."

"Hmm," we say to her at the side of the room. "I see what you mean. What if you and I talk about the story as a way of modeling how readers don't just identify and accept an author's message point blank. They think about whether it holds any meaning or actual relevance for them, and they wonder how it might or might not inform how they live their own lives."

Eager to not reduce the act of reading to the dismissive assigning of adages, the teacher immediately agrees, and so we sit in front of the students with copies of "The Sun and the Wind" in our hands. We begin by first sharing how we noticed the pronouns in the text, which allow us to comprehend that the sun is a "she" and the wind is a "he." That, in turn, makes us wonder whether Aesop might also be suggesting that women are stronger than men, or at least that the kind of gentle persuasion usually associated with women is more powerful than the more aggressive tactics associated with men. Despite the fact that we are women, we aren't quite sure we agree with that. We find ourselves thinking about our parents, another "she" and "he" pair, who, like the sun and the wind in the story, had different ideas about how to get us, as children, to do things they wanted us to do. We delve into this idea in front of the students, each of us sharing memories of different times growing up when one parent was more likely to strong-arm us, as the wind in the fable did, while the other used subtler means. But that makes us think of something else that we say to students: how much we hated being manipulated—as we realize, through talking, the man in the story has been. What if he was supposed to be somewhere important? What if he had things to do? Was the sun even thinking about that, or was she just toying with the man, getting him to do what she wanted him to do, without any concern for his feelings? Might that, in the end, not seem worse than the wind, who at least was upfront about what he wanted?

By this point the rug is a sea of hands waving wildly in the air. Although our intention has been to model how readers can talk back to a text to consider and reflect on what they make of its message, we realize that these students, who love to talk, are eager to join in the conversation. Before we open the floor, however, we want to make one final point, which is to model how readers can take different aspects of a text and turn those ideas inward to consider themselves in a new light. We tell the students this and jump in, wondering aloud whether we, as teachers and as parents, are like the sun or the wind, and either way, how we might sometimes abuse the power we have, using persuasion or strength to make a point or get our way. We talk back and forth for a few moments about whether and when these means might be justified, and we then bring our discussion to a close by recognizing that this story has shown us that we need to be more aware of when and how we use the power we have so we don't end up being like the sun or the wind, toying with others by flexing our power just to prove that we can.

We then put the students in groups of three so that everyone has a chance to talk, and as they begin, we look out at the groups. We see kids talking richly, listening and responding, and we marvel at how layered even a fable can become if we truly approach it as meaning-making readers.

What We Do as Readers

WE KNOW THE PROCESS OF READING DOESN'T END
WHEN WE COME TO THE FINAL PAGE

As we think about what happens to readers after they finish a text, it is interesting to note that Dr. Seuss' beloved classic *The Cat in the Hat* (1957)—a book that is usually used to introduce children to the delights of reading and to practice decoding—ends with a question for his readers. When the mother comes home, unaware of the havoc the Cat in the Hat has created, she asks her children what they did that day. Sally and her brother look at each other, unsure of just what to say: "Should we tell her about it? Now what SHOULD we do? Well . . . What would YOU do if your mother asked you?" (p. 61). This is, in effect, an invitation to engage in evaluation, to bring the text back to your own life and consider the implications of the story for yourself in a way that might ultimately shed some light on what kind of person you are or could be and what you made of the text. Dr. Seuss seems to know that this is as much a part of reading as decoding the 220 rhyming words or delighting in the cat's shenanigans, and he builds it right into a text he has written for the youngest emergent readers.

We acknowledged this part of the process as well when we took a closer look at what we mean by meaning making in Chapter 2: Readers don't simply close one book and immediately open another, as these third graders initially did. Even amid our busy lives we pause to take stock of what we've read, sometimes letting the words burrow deep inside us where the text can live a sort of second life, as part of our own experience, other times questioning what an author is saying because what we've come to understand doesn't quite add up. The teachers in our workshop did the former when they found themselves thinking of Susan Marie Scavo's poem as they recalled their mothers or looked around their classrooms, newly aware or reminded of how subjective each person's perspective is. Our third graders, on the other hand, joined us in the latter as they, too, began to consider whether Aesop's message was perhaps too simple, and to then explore thoughts and ideas that might underlie that message.

In both cases, though, the process of evaluation allowed these readers to take away something meaningful from the text—even though, in the case of the fable, that meaning was ultimately based on challenging, not accepting, Aesop's message. They also both engaged in the process once they had constructed an understanding of the text's ideas and themes. This is critical because, as Alfred Tatum notes, "It is difficult to value (or reject) something you have not fully experienced" (p. 29). We believe, however, that the inverse is also true: that it is difficult to fully experience something if you haven't considered its value, asking yourself some variation of Dr. Seuss's question: What would you do—and why?

WE DON'T WAIT TILL WE'VE REACHED THE END TO THINK

We hold off evaluating a text until we reach the end so as to first fully consider what the whole, as well as the parts, might be saying. But we don't defer all our thinking till then. We think deeply as we make our way through a text, as the students in the previous chapters were doing, trying always, as Maxine Greene advises, "to notice what there is to be noticed" (1995, p. 125). This, put simply, is what it means to fully experience a text. In the above example, for instance, when we jumped in to model a discussion on the spur of the moment, we didn't rely on what we remembered about the text from past readings. We took a few minutes instead to reread it, noting the small details, the "she" and the "he" and the fact that the man they chose for their contest had been called a traveler, which suggested that he was on his way somewhere, with perhaps a purpose of his own that differed from the sun's and the wind's. We reacquainted ourselves with the particulars, as well as with the whole, grounding ourselves in the details of the text instead of in whatever general memory still lingered in our minds.

We fear, however, that the third graders had gone into the text not to consider all that it held, attentive to both large and small details, but to extract the main idea, which they seemingly yanked out of the fable like a fish on a hook to display, trophy-like, in the room. And we fear, as well, that they do this because we've taught them to. Once again, we sometimes end our instruction at identification, rather than seeing that as a step toward some deeper purpose, which limits what even precocious and highly verbal children are able to take away. And whether we actually mean to or not, we send out a message that reading is about "stamping" texts with a single, fixed idea, which reduces their complexity and makes the experience of reading far less than it can be.

OUR ASSESSMENT OF A TEXT'S WORTH OFTEN BEGINS WITH A GUT RESPONSE

Many years ago Lucy Calkins (1997) made the astute observation that when we, as readers, finish a book, we don't immediately want to rush out and create a diorama. Instead we want to talk to someone, ideally another reader who's read the same book. For many of us that comment changed how we thought about end-of-text work, as we moved away from arts-and-crafts projects to more authentic responses. Similarly though, when we finish a book, we don't as readers want to rush out and do many of the items that are frequently listed on the menus of options for responding to texts, such as writing a letter to the character or scripting an alternative ending to a book. Some of these options may, indeed, help us to think more deeply about a text, though without additional scaffolding or contextualizing—especially around authentic purposes of reading— these responses are often disappointing, with insight into the text or the reader appearing by happenstance.

Instead, as readers, we tend to think about our basic reactions: Did we like or not like the book, and, in either case, *why?* The reasons why we did or didn't like a text often touch on many of the literary elements that are visible in our classrooms: We liked or didn't like the characters because they respectively felt real or inauthentic; we liked or didn't like the way it was written, that is, we responded to the voice, style, or tone; and, as we discussed in the previous chapter, we liked or didn't like a book because of the direction it ultimately took—i.e., we responded to the plot or to what we perceived to be the author's concerns. All of these responses impact what we do or don't take away from a text. They contribute to our sense of value. But they all require a follow-up step in which we question and consider how these initial likes and dislikes reveal something about who we are and how we see the world. They help define us, which is one of the functions and outcomes of evaluation.

EVALUATION CAN ALSO TOUCH ON THE DEEPER REASONS FOR READING

Additionally, why we did or didn't like a book often speaks to the bigger purposes of reading, with evaluation opening the door for us to consider how we've been impacted, and perhaps even changed or affirmed, through our experience with a text. We like or dislike a book, for instance, according to how well it did what Anna Quindlen (2007) says in her foreword to *A Wrinkle in Time* is the true benefit of reading: that "the most memorable books . . . make us feel less alone, convince us that our own foibles and quirks are both as individual as a finger-print and as universal as an open hand" (p. 1). We like a book, thus, because we sense some truth or recognition of ourselves in it; we see something universal in the singular specifics, even if the book doesn't explore something we've experienced. And feeling that we aren't the only ones going through whatever turmoil, confusion, or isolation we may be living through allows us sometimes to forgive ourselves or put our own troubles in perspective.

Similarly, we may like a book because it gives voice to something that we'd sensed or perceived but had never been able to articulate before. Thus, we can like a book because a writer has movingly captured in words something we've felt but haven't been able to actually name, and now having it named we go forth in the world with more awareness and understanding. Bringing evaluation more visibly into our classrooms gives us an opportunity to give voice to the way that texts let us feel validated and less alone. And naming that for children allows them to go forth with more awareness of the role books can play in their lives.

WE SET THE IDEAS WE UNCOVER IN TEXTS NEXT TO OUR OWN EXPERIENCE TO DRAFT AND REVISE THE "TEXT" OF OUR LIVES

As we made visible to these third-grade students, once we have fully experienced a text and constructed an understanding of what we think it may be saying, we hold that understanding up to our own life to see how it compares with what we've already experienced. And we consider how the invisible ideas we've ultimately been able to "see" in the text might impact and affect our own lives.

We could say that we're making text-to-self connections, though they have a particular purpose here, and they come at a particular place in the reading process, *after* we've constructed an understanding of the themes an author is exploring. Additionally, these connections ask us specifically to think about how an abstraction, such as the author's message or theme, might affirm or challenge or add to our lives, which pushes students beyond connections about literal or surface elements in the text in a way that stretches their thinking. These connections also necessitate reflection, without which we risk blundering from book to book and experience to experience without, as our epigraph author, Edmund Burke, might say, deriving any nourishment.

We might better and more accurately describe this process by saying that we are using our understanding of the text, and the details from which that understanding was constructed, to draft and revise our sense of ourselves and the world around us. For just as a text unfolds over time, so do our lives. We grow and change and evolve and develop with each new experience we have, including those we have with texts that we've experienced fully. Evaluation allows us to reflect on how we are developing, as thinkers, as readers, as human beings. It asks us to think not just about what the character learned, but what we may have learned, too. And, once we've considered Dr. Seuss's question, "Now what would you do if this happened to you?," evaluation asks us to pose the same question we'd ask of characters: What kind of person would do that or think that? What do our actions, our dreams, and our feelings say about who we are?

WE FOCUS ON THE DETAILS OF THE TEXT RATHER THAN ON "CRITICAL LENSES"

Finally, in our Aesop example, we touched on a few ideas that are often taught in the framework of "critical lenses" or "critical literacy," which engages students in thinking about issues of social justice as they read (Bomer and Bomer 2001;

McLaughlin and DeVoogd 2004). We considered, for example, what the text might be saying about gender roles and power as we noticed the pronouns, and we thought about what perspectives were missing when we wondered about the traveler. These are lenses that are taught in a variety of ways, depending on the age of the students, but it's important to note that, similar to all the work we've described in this book, we didn't come to the text with a predetermined lens or purpose. Rather, we employed these lenses because of the details that we noticed and considered in the text.

We do believe that critical lenses can be useful in certain situations, but we must be aware that by arming students with those lenses, we may, in a sense, be frontloading or handing them a theme, a theme that they themselves actually need to construct—and critique—through the details of the text. And we must be careful that, in the guise of providing students with higher-level critical-thinking tools, we are not inadvertently nudging them, once again, to our own meaning or perspective. Similarly, we want to make sure we're not limiting, but rather expanding, what they see in a text, so that, like our third graders intent on extracting the fable's main idea, our students aren't casting their rods into the depths of a text to reel in an idea about gender roles or power, for example, while ignoring everything else. Instead, we want them to construct their ideas from the bottom up, rather than using the top-down approach that critical lenses can foster.

With all this in mind, we aim to make visible the following to students:

* The purpose of reading ultimately rests in what the reader takes from the text.

* Once readers have constructed an understanding of what they think a text is "about," they consider whether that holds any weight or relevance for their life.

* Readers draw on the same details they used to construct an understanding of the text to draft and revise an understanding of themselves and the world around them.

What This Looks Like in Classrooms

In each of the classrooms we've looked at in the previous chapters—with our third graders reading *How to Steal a Dog*, our fourth graders tackling *A Taste of Blackberries*, our fifth graders thinking about *Pictures of Hollis Woods*, and our seventh graders deep into *Miracle's Boys*—we set aside a period or two to explicitly engage in evaluation.

What we do as teachers: *We carve out time for evaluation.*

We introduce this part of the meaning-making process by sharing with children what may be the ultimate reading secret: that we actually read not just to think about what the character learned or what the author might be trying to say, but to think about how those lessons and ideas might impact and inform our own lives. We can do this because, when we read deeply, fully experiencing a text as we have with all these various classes, we've shared the experiences we've read about, as if we've had them ourselves. We've been moved or saddened, emboldened or regretful, as the characters have, facing hard choices or overcoming obstacles. And knowing that "experience is the best teacher," we want to make sure that we take some time to think about what we learned.

We model this by sharing with each class what we took away from the text in the most authentic way possible. With *How to Steal a Dog*, Barbara O'Connor's book about Georgina, the girl who hoped to help her family out by ransoming a dog she had kidnapped, we talk about how often we do what the class had come to see Georgina and her family doing—brushing aside or dismissing both our own and our family's feelings in order to just get through the day—and how we want to change that dynamic by making sure we take more time to listen and talk to each other. With *A Taste of Blackberries*, the book where our nameless narrator lost his best friend Jamie, we share how the book reminded us that death can sometimes strike unexpectedly and that, knowing that, we want to try to value our friends and loved ones while they're here among us, avoiding the kind of petty annoyances and irritations that can tarnish relationships. With *Pictures of Hollis Woods*, which recounted an orphaned girl's difficult journey to find a family and a home, we talk about how—despite how very different we are from Hollis, who was bumped around various foster homes, gaining a reputation for trouble—we still recognize ourselves in her, in particular the way she was all too ready to take the blame for things that had nothing to do with her. Seeing that, we want to make sure we take the time to see the bigger picture, as Hollis did when she laid out all the pictures she'd drawn and realized that she wasn't responsible for everything that happened—and she wasn't doomed to always be bad. And, finally, with *Miracle's Boys*, Jacqueline Woodson's book about the brothers coping with the death of their parents, we find ourselves questioning one of the ideas the class thinks Jacqueline Woodson is exploring: that keeping a family together is worth more than an individual's dream. We think about Ty'ree, the oldest brother, who gave up his dream of going to college to keep his family intact, and we wish that the world could be the kind of place where people didn't have to make those kinds of sacrifices. And we wondered what we would have done in his shoes. Would we have made the same choice? And if not, what does that say about us?

What we do as teachers: *We model how we make meaning through evaluation.*

Then with each class's big ideas chart positioned for all to see, we ask the students to take a few minutes to jot down their thoughts about what they think they might have learned about themselves or about people in general. Then we push back the desks to form a circle and hold an accountable talk, a discussion that the students conduct themselves, to share and build and deepen their ideas with minimum input or prompting from us.

What we do as teachers: *We let students talk before we ask for formal responses or essays.*

How to Steal a Dog brought home for every student in the room the consequences of lying and the need to listen to that voice inside your head that is telling you you're doing something wrong. But many students pushed themselves further. One student, for instance, went on to say, "If you're lying to someone, you're actually lying to yourself," while another concluded, "I think the whole book isn't just about lying, but about saying what you need to say." Many students also returned to a particular line that they felt was significant— "The more you stir it, the more it stinks"—which a secondary character who acts as something of a mentor to Georgina said. Many felt that this line made them see how lies beget more lies—or, as one student said, "The more you do something bad, the more you're going to feel bad." And one student brought that right into her life, just as the teachers in our workshop did with Susan Marie Scavo's poem: "When Mookie said, 'The more you stir it, the more it stinks,'" she shared, "I thought of my sister. When I fight with her, I get a little sadder every time."

A Taste of Blackberries made many of the fourth graders, like David and Jose, the two boys who kept hoping until the very last page that Jamie was not really dead, newly aware of how deep loss is and how it can be expressed—and even denied. Some students felt affirmed by this as they too had experienced a death of someone close; others related the loss in the story to other losses they had experienced—an absent father, a cousin no longer living nearby. Some found consolation in the idea that even when someone you love has died, they can live on in your heart. And a few even saw some hope in the fact that while the narrator no longer had Jamie, he seemed to push beyond the guilt he felt at being still alive when he delivered a basket of blackberries to Jamie's mom, which she accepted with deep thanks and love. Several students also extended on our idea, pledging to try to not get so worked up when a friend goofed off or was annoying—and to not assume that a friend was clowning, as the narrator had done when Jamie collapsed after being stung by a bee, without making sure first that the friend was all right.

The fifth graders who read *Pictures of Hollis Woods* were impacted by the book in numerous ways. Some children focused on how seemingly willing Hollis was to accept other people's opinion of her as a troublemaker, and they hoped to go forth into the world remembering, as one student said, that "you have to always believe in yourself and not let others bring you down." Picking up on the same thread in the text, another student offered a slightly different variation: "I'm going to try to see what's good in people instead of always thinking about the bad." Other students focused on the way Hollis continually seemed to be talking to other people in her head. "I thought I was the only person who did that," one student said, touching on the way that books can make us feel less alone. "But now I think that those voices aren't really other people. They're different sides of me, and I have to figure out which one to listen to, the good one or the bad." And another built on what we had said: "I'm going to try to remember that people have their own reasons for doing things. It's not always about me."

Finally, our seventh graders thought long and hard about *Miracle's Boys*. Many of the students identified with Newcharlie, the middle brother who, we learn, was sent to a juvenile detention center because he had tried to hold up a candy store to help his mother pay the bills. Several students thought about how they themselves sometimes do bad things for good reasons, and they needed to remember that, as one of the students said, "a good reason doesn't make a bad thing right." They also wanted to remember that actions carry consequences, which can change the course of a life: "You can't always control things," one student said. "Things can get out of hand." Some also harked back to a pattern they'd noticed around recurring details that involved the word *freedom*, particularly to a passage in which the boys' mother suggests to Lafayette that "being free means you help somebody else get free." They thought about whether they were free, and if so, how they might or should use their freedom and how they might balance the freedom they craved with their responsibility to others.

With each class we listened as the students shared their thoughts, noticing all the different ways they evaluated the text, and we saved a few minutes at the end of the session to name and chart for them what they did. Since individual students arrived at meaning through different and varied means, the list of the ways we evaluate a text took a slightly different form in each classroom. (See Figure 7–1, p. 190, for sample chart.) But across the rooms we saw children thinking about what a single line might have to say to them and how they might do things differently in their own lives now that they had experienced something vicariously in a text. We saw children feeling less alone because something in the text affirmed what they'd thought or felt or done themselves. We saw children appreciating their own lives more or wanting to be more tolerant and forgiving of others than they'd been before. Additionally, in every class, we saw children who were readers, children who had kept their minds open and attentive to what a text might have to say and who were then able to consider whether that had any relevance in their lives. They were children who had made meaning, in the deepest possible way, and who left the classroom after the discussion more thoughtful and self-aware.

What we do as teachers: *We notice and name what children are doing to create an evolving anchor chart.*

What We Do as Teachers

WE CARVE OUT TIME FOR EVALUATION

While this point may seem obvious, the sad fact is that all too often this vital step is relegated to the sidelines in classrooms, with a student occasionally writing an entry in his or her reader's notebook about how a book affected them or another taking issue with an author's idea. This may be because we deem it too personal to warrant classroom time. Or perhaps because, in our assessment- and data-driven age, we're not quite sure how to measure it or even how to teach it, other than to name it for students and invite them into the process. Yet we're reminded here of Vicki Spandel, whose wise words in the preface of *The 9 Rights of Every Writers* apply not just to writing, but reading:

> At its best, assessment can enormously enhance instruction by helping us identify both problems and strengths that might otherwise go undiscovered. At its best, instruction can give us insights not only about content but about ourselves. But assessment must focus on what matters, not on what's easy to measure. . . . And instruction must go well beyond anything assessment can effectively measure to those deeper reasons for [reading]. We must choose to take it to that level. (pp. xii-xiii)

We choose to make time for evaluation because we believe it touches at the heart of those deeper reasons for reading. We choose to build it into the routines and rituals of the classrooms we work in. And we choose to assess our students not just by the skills we can easily measure on a right-answer test or a reading-level letter, but on how they are growing and thinking as readers and what they're taking away from what they read.

Rethinking our practice: *We provide time at the end of every whole-class read-aloud book for students to consider what they're taking away from it.*

WE MODEL HOW WE MAKE MEANING THROUGH EVALUATION

As discussed before, we usually try to keep our modeling to a minimum. We use it sparingly because it can have the inadvertent effect of casting us in the role of experts who produce definitive readings of texts and also because students are more likely to grasp the mind-work of reading if we orchestrate scaffolded scenarios for them in which they can actively construct meaning. Here, though, we modeled our own thoughts and ideas. We do so during the process of evaluation because we are not producing readings of the text at this point; instead, we are drafting the text of our own lives. We are showing students how we use what we read to revise and hone and construct an understanding of ourselves and the human experience. Provided we do so authentically—sharing how a text has moved or challenged us, how it has forced us to rethink our assumptions or absorb new realizations—the benefits of modeling are vast. It lets children see us questioning and reflecting, grappling with ambivalence and, at times, being vulnerable in ways that ultimately encourage them, in turn, to take risks in their thinking. Above all, it conveys the enduring understanding that is foundational to all our teaching: that we read, in the end, to live.

Of course, as can happen whenever we model, we run the risk of children piggybacking on our thoughts rather than developing their own. Yet because evaluation is so highly personal, children often come up with unique particulars even when they latch onto something we've said. Thus one third grader who'd read *How to Steal a Dog* echoed our desire to communicate better with our families, vowing to try not to shrug or say "Nothing" the next time his parents ask what happened in school. And several seventh graders found themselves asking the same question we raised about sacrificing their dreams, though most of them thought they would ultimately make the same choice that Ty'ree did, believing that there would be time for college later and that deferred dreams can be reclaimed.

Rethinking our practice: *We purposely reveal ourselves as questioning and uncertain, to encourage students to take risks.*

WE LET STUDENTS TALK BEFORE WE ASK FOR FORMAL RESPONSES OR ESSAYS

We also discussed earlier our belief that, as Ralph Peterson and Maryann Eeds put it, "Dialogue is the best pedagogy" (2007, p. 26). Not only does talk here deepen students' sense of all the various ways a reader can find meaning in a text, it allows each student to develop a vision of this part of the process—to "see" what it means to make meaning—so that when they are asked to commit their thoughts to paper, they have a deeper understanding of what meaning making could actually look and sound like.

Too often, however, we ask students to write without this deeper vision, which frequently means that students' work falls along the ability fault line or divide, with students who come to our classrooms with certain understandings already in place doing well, and students who come without those understandings doing poorly. Additionally, the rubrics for our essay assignments and our standardized tests tend to evaluate students on how well they've argued a point, not on how authentic or personally meaningful the point they're making is. In this way we send a message to our students that we value rhetoric, logic, and organization more than meaningful content. In fact, such rubrics can encourage students to choose a particular position or stand according to which one they can best support, regardless of whether it is actually something they think or feel or not.

We do, of course, need to teach children how to express themselves in written language that is clear and focused and organized, but this is far, far easier to do once they have something meaningful to say, which they often arrive at more effectively through talk. We may also want to teach them to defend a position that they don't really hold, as a way of both recognizing someone else's perspective and building their rhetorical skills. But neither of these supports the goal of creating lifelong readers who continue to read once they leave our rooms because they've come to deeply value what reading can do for them. So we need to be clear about what purposes are served by the things we ask students to do—and make those purposes clear to students as well, balancing the need to help students master skills with the need to invite them into the deeper and more meaningful reasons to read. Otherwise we risk raising children who value structure over content and proving a point over opening their minds to something you hadn't yet considered.

> **Rethinking our practice:** *We make sure our written assignments are aligned to and reflect our deepest purposes and always let students talk before they write.*

WE NOTICE AND NAME WHAT STUDENTS ARE DOING TO CREATE EVOLVING ANCHOR CHARTS

As we have at every step throughout the meaning-making process, we notice and name what the students are doing as a way of making visible and explicit the complicated work of reading. And we also create anchor charts that capture the thinking work they've done as readers so as to support them in transferring that work from one text to the next. Many of these charts evolve over time as we add new ways we notice the students using to make meaning of what they read. And the charts we create to support evaluation typically remain up all year long as a way of honoring and keeping our deepest, most enduring goals of reading highly visible. The chart below (Figure 7–1) reflects the various ways students take texts into their lives over the course of a year. We add bullet points as they come up in the students' discussions and written work, using the students' own words and language whenever possible.

Digging Deeper into Books
Strategies We Use to Consider What a Text Means to Us
▶ Think about whether or not–and why–we'd do the same thing that a character did. What does that say about who we are and how we view the world?
▶ Consider whether anything in the text made us think about doing something different in our own lives.
▶ Think about what a single line might have to say about our own lives.
▶ Think about whether the text expressed something that we'd felt but had never been able to put into words or completely understand before.
▶ Consider whether the text made us see our own lives in a new light.
▶ Think about whether the text made us see other people or the world in a new light.

Figure 7–1. A co-created summary chart naming the ways we evaluate a text's worth

Making Every Student's Thinking Visible

SUPPORTING EVALUATION IN AN INDEPENDENT
READING CONFERENCE

As teachers who value independence, we must always think long and hard about what we need to do to help students transfer knowledge gained from one experience to another and from one text to the next. And while the above lesson goes far toward making visible a part of the process of meaning making that often remains unseen, we anticipate that students may need multiple exposures and opportunities to engage in evaluation before they regularly do it on their own. So just as we attempt to confer with students when they open the first page of a book, we seek out those who've reached the last page in order to ask what the book meant to them before it's returned to the library shelf and another is pulled and checked out.

Here, for instance, we confer with seventh-grade Nakayla who has just finished David Pelzer's often grisly memoir of his abusive childhood, *A Child*

Called "It" (1993). When we spoke with her last, Nakayla had been reading hoping to learn more about why a mother would do such a thing to a child. She knew the mother was an alcoholic, but she wasn't sure this fully explained the pain she inflicted on her son, and picking up and attending to a few details about the mother's failed relationship with her husband, she'd had a hunch that the mother's abuse might be a way of getting back at David's father. When we talked to her, however, she was beginning to question that idea because, as she continued to read on, she noticed that the father was mentioned less and less. And so we'd left her with the suggestion that she might need to look for other patterns that might give her different ideas.

Now, as we sidle up to her, we ask her what she'd thought of the book.

"It was really incredible," she says. "I read it faster than any book I've ever read before because I really couldn't put it down."

"That's what I hear a lot of readers say. It's both horrible and amazing. But I'm wondering, do you think it made you think anything about your own life, the way that *Miracle's Boys* did?"

"Well," she says, "it definitely made me feel lucky that my mom wasn't like David's. I mean she yells at me sometimes and she's even grounded me, but compared to what David's mom did, that's nothing."

"A lot of books make us look back at our lives with a new appreciation," we say, naming for her both how texts work and what she's just done as a reader. "So it's great that maybe *A Child Called 'It'* put your relationship with your mom into some kind of perspective."

"Yeah," she said. "That is what it did. But . . ." she begins, then pauses. "You know how I was hoping to find an explanation for why the mom did all those things? Well, I never really found anything else. There didn't seem to be any pattern to it. She just did these awful things for no reason. And while I really, really loved the book, I don't like the idea that there wasn't a reason for her doing those horrible things. I wanted to try to understand it and I feel like I couldn't."

"Well," we say, "it could be because you were more interested in that than the author was. Maybe David Pelzer was too busy trying to show us how he survived to think about why this was happening. Or maybe there was no reason. It was just the way the mom was."

"Maybe," Nakayla says. "But I don't like the idea that awful things can just happen, anytime, no matter what you do."

"No, I agree, I don't like that either. It actually makes me kind of scared. But maybe this means that you learned something else, something about you. Maybe you're the kind of person who believes that people do things for a reason and you like finding out and thinking about those reasons because it helps you understand them, even if you don't like what they're doing. Do you think that's possible?"

"Sort of, yeah. I mean I guess I am like that, even though I never thought that before."

"And maybe that's something to think about when you choose another book. Maybe you'd like a book that offers more explanations than A *Child Called 'It,'* a book that looks at the why's, not just the what's. Do you think we should go over and see what we can find?"

"Yeah," Nakayla says, getting up from her desk.

And so we make our way to the library and help Nakayla browse through the baskets. We pull out *Cut* by Patricia McCormick (2000) and *Stop Pretending* by Sonya Sones (1999), *Journey* by Patricia MacLachlan (1991), and our old friend *Hollis Woods*. And as we watch Nakayla take them back to her desk to thumb through the pages and read the back covers and sample a paragraph or two, we think we see a student who has visibly grown, taken a step toward whatever future she will ultimately forge for herself by an interacting with words on a page in one of those "small, flat, rigid squares of paper" that we're deeply grateful for.

Rethinking How We Teach Reading	
What We Used to Do . . .	**What We Do Now . . .**
We used to move from read-aloud to read-aloud without ever explicitly asking students what they were taking away from the text.	We make sure to devote time for evaluation in order to bring the process of reading and meaning making to its fullest and deepest end.
We used to have students write reading responses without letting them first explore their thoughts through talk.	We build in time for students to talk before assigning written work (with the occasional exception of test-related assignments).
We used to provide students with a menu of options for responding in writing to their reading without fully articulating–for ourselves or to them– our purposes.	We always try to align written assignments to authentic and meaningful purposes so as not to turn assignments into tasks that some students see no purpose in.
We used to model whatever strategy or task we asked of students with every minilesson.	We keep our modeling to a minimum, except during evaluation when we model in order to demonstrate how we draft and revise our understanding of ourselves, not just of a text.
We used to ask students to consider questions of power, fairness, social justice, and perspective as they read as a way of developing critical literacy.	We prefer to let students explore those issues as the natural outcome of engaging and thinking deeply about the implications of the story, without frontloading those ideas first.

Learning From the Texts That Are Our Classrooms

. . . Through reading we are given words and through words we gain the power to subdue chaos and tame storms. Reading gives us back to ourselves in a way nothing else and no one else can. Ultimately it enables us to say yes, yes—and then continue on with the mystery of this journey we call our lives.

—Julius Lester

We return here where we started in Chapter 1, looking on as our friend's second-grade daughter, Mara, asks her mother to explain the meaning of the campaign poster, "Vote or Die." That was a moment that got us reflecting on how students seem to be learning that meaning resides outside of themselves. After reading this book, which has focused mainly on narrative writing, you may wonder why we chose to open it with an anecdote about a child reading a piece of nonfiction. The truth is, we often think of that moment with Mara, not only when we're working with students inside their classrooms but also when we watch them leave, streaming out of the buildings and into the rest of their lives—lives filled with lyrics and text messages, video games and Facebook posts, basketball moves and violin fingerings.

The fact is, the lives of our students are their texts. And while we surely hope that as a result of our work, some of our students will become lovers of books and turn to them the way we do, we take as our mandate as teachers and as teachers of teachers something larger: that each of our students will leave our classrooms knowing that meaning is theirs to make. No one should cede this power to someone else—whether that someone is a parent, a friend, a teacher, or the media—nor should they cede this power to the text itself. If we can show each and every student, through our language, attitudes, and instruction, that meaning is a construct, something made out of something they notice, we are confident they will notice more deeply, read in more engaged ways—and come back for more.

Our lives, of course, are also *our* texts, and in the course of writing this book, as we have reflected on what it means to read and what it means to teach, we have noticed how similar the work of reading is to the work of teaching. Each strand of ourselves, the teacher and the reader, notices what's to be noticed. From that we draft and revise our way toward some deeper understanding—of a book when we read, and of the needs of our students when we teach. And just as we've seen that readers don't sit back expecting meaning to happen outside ourselves, so, too, as teachers we make meaning in active and engaged ways. We don't just look at the summaries of our students' thoughts, the data available from formal assessments, but also at what they do and say as they are in the midst of reading—these are the details, in effect, that we use to construct our meaning.

In order to do this, we need to first create opportunities for students to get inside of texts and then we need to get out of the way and listen. Unfortunately, listening is extremely hard to do—in life, yes, but especially in classrooms. Think of that loudspeaker over every door and of the telephone lurking in the corner, and now think of those as metaphors. We work in environments that interrupt us, that talk over us, that tell us in so many ways that what they have to say is more important than whatever is going on in our classrooms. In fact, we'll go so far as to say that we work in environments that devalue listening, that have taught us *not* to listen or, perhaps more accurately, to listen *for* . . . the right answer, rather than listening *to* . . . our students as they think.

We have tried, in this book, to show some ways to organize instruction that allows us to listen, to notice what's to be noticed in our classrooms. This is the vital work we have to do as teachers, for each student who crosses our path is in the process of forging an identity, not only as a reader of books but as a reader of their world. Showing them what agency looks and sounds like while making meaning in a text—to notice what's to be noticed and make something of it—is a microcosm for what that can look and sound like while making meaning in their lives.

So, too, we are forging our identities as teachers each time we step inside a classroom. We can hand that process over to someone else—a prepackaged curriculum or teacher guide, an assessment or a standard—or we can become agents in that process, composing our lives by composing meaning from the texts that are our classrooms, just as books have taught us we can.

Appendix

Appendix 1

A two-column KNOW/WONDER chart to help

students keep track of their thinking

What We Know	What We Wonder

© 2012 by Dorothy Barnhouse and Vicki Vinton from *What Readers Really Do*. Portsmouth, NH: Heinemann

Appendix 2

Chart for tracking a pattern

Patterns We Notice	Where They Occur

© 2012 by Dorothy Barnhouse and Vicki Vinton from *What Readers Really Do*. Portsmouth, NH: Heinemann

Appendix 3

Chart for connecting patterns to think about possible ideas being shown in a book

What We Know (Patterns We Notice)	Other Patterns This Might Connect With ___ + ___ + ___	What We Wonder (Ideas These Connections Might be Showing) = ___?

© 2012 by Dorothy Barnhouse and Vicki Vinton from *What Readers Really Do*. Portsmouth, NH: Heinemann

Appendix 4

Growing the KNOW/WONDER chart to draft interpretations

about changing patterns in books

What We Know (How Is Pattern Changing?)	What We Wonder	What We Think ("Maybe Statements")

© 2012 by Dorothy Barnhouse and Vicki Vinton from *What Readers Really Do*. Portsmouth, NH: Heinemann

Works Cited

Ackerman, Diane. 1991. "White Lanterns." *The Writer on Her Work*, ed. Janet Sternburg. Vol. 2. New York: W. W. Norton.

Beers, Kylene. 2002. *When Kids Can't Read: What Teachers Can Do.* Portsmouth, NH: Heinemann.

Blau, Sheridan D. 2003. *The Literature Workshop: Teaching Texts and Their Readers.* Portsmouth, NH: Boynton/Cook.

Bomer, Randy. 1995. *Time for Meaning: Crafting Literate Lives in Middle & High School.* Portsmouth, NH: Heinemann.

Bomer, Randy, and Katherine Bomer. 2001. *For a Better World: Reading and Writing for Social Justice.* Portsmouth, NH: Heinemann.

Bunting, Eve. 1991. *Fly Away Home.* New York: Clarion Books.

Burroway, Janet. 2003. *Writing Fiction: A Guide to Narrative Craft.* White Plains, NY: Pearson Longman.

Calkins, Lucy McCormick. 1997. "Get Real About Reading." *Scholastic Instructor.* May 1. Print.

Danziger, Paula. 1910, 1997. *Amber Brown Sees Red.* New York: Puffin Books.

Dewey, John. 1997. *How We Think.* Toronto: Dover Publications.

DiCamillo, Kate. 2000. *Because of Winn-Dixie.* Somerville, MA: Candlewick Press.

Dillard, Annie. 1989. *The Writing Life.* New York: HarperCollins.

Ellmann, Richard. 1983. *James Joyce.* Revised ed. New York: Oxford University Press.

Fountas, Irene, and Gay Su Pinnell. 1996. *Guided Reading: Good First Teaching for All Children*. Portsmouth, NH: Heinemann.

Gardner, John. 1984. *The Art of Fiction*. New York: Alfred A. Knopf.

Giff, Patricia Reilly. 1984. *Fish Face*. New York: Random House.

_____. 2002. *Pictures of Hollis Woods*. New York: Random House.

Glover, Matt, and Mary Alice Berry. 2011. "I Can't Know But I Can Project: Planning Units of Study in the Writing Workshop." *Heinemann Catalog-Journal*, Spring: 16–19. Print.

Green, Elizabeth. "Building a Better Teacher." 2010. *The New York Times Sunday Magazine*, March 7: 30+.

Greene, Maxine. 1988. *The Dialectic of Freedom*. New York: Teachers College Press.

_____. 1995. *Releasing the Imagination: Essays on Education, the Arts, and Social Change*. San Francisco: Jossey-Bass.

Hesse, Karen. 1999. *Just Juice*. New York: Scholastic.

Hopkins, Ellen. 2008. *Identical*. New York: Margaret K. McElderry Books.

Hunter, Erin. 2007. *Warriors: The New Prophecy: Sunset*. New York: HarperCollins.

Johnston, Peter. 2004. *Choice Words*. Portland, ME: Stenhouse Publishers.

Keene, Ellin. 2008. *To Understand*. Portsmouth, NH: Heinemann.

Konigsburg, E. L. 1967. *From the Mixed-Up Files of Mrs. Basil E. Frankweiler*. New York: Simon & Schuster.

Kundera, Milan. 2007. *The Curtain: An Essay in Seven Parts*. New York: HarperCollins.

Lamott, Anne. 1995. *Bird by Bird*. New York: Pantheon Books.

Levine, Gail Carson. 1997. *Ella Enchanted*. New York: HarperCollins.

MacLachlan, Patricia. 1991. *Journey*. New York: Random House Children's Books.

_____. 1994. *Skylark*. New York: HarperCollins Children's Books.

Maclean, Norman. 1976. *A River Runs Through It and Other Stories*. Chicago: University of Chicago Press.

McCormick, Patricia. 2000. *Cut*. New York: Scholastic.

McDonald, Megan. 2000. *Judy Moody Was in a Mood. Not a Good Mood. A Bad Mood*. Somerville, MA: Candlewick Press.

McLaughlin, Maureen, and Glenn L. DeVoogd. 2004. *Critical Literacy: Enhancing Students' Comprehension of a Text*. New York: Scholastic.

Merriam, Eve. 2000. "The First Day of Spring." *Songs of Myself: An Anthology of Poems and Art*, ed. Georgia Heard. New York: Mondo Publishing.

Murray, Donald. 1985. *A Writer Teaches Writing*. Boston: Houghton Mifflin.

Myers, Walter Dean. 2008. *Game*. New York: HarperTeen.

Neri, Greg. 2009. "Writing About Serious Topics for Teens." Schoolwide Fundamentals. Accessed July 1, 2010 www.schoolwidefundamentals.com/post/2009/09/03/Writing-about-serious-topics-for-teens.aspx.

O'Connor, Barbara. 2007. *How to Steal a Dog*. New York: Farrar, Straus & Giroux.

O'Connor, Flannery. 1969. *Mysteries and Manners: Occasional Prose*. New York: Farrar, Straus & Giroux.

Pelzer, David. 1993. *A Child Called "It": One Child's Courage to Survive*. Omaha, NE: Omaha Press.

Peterson, Ralph, and Maryann Eeds. 2007. *Grand Conversations: Literature Groups in Action*. New York: Scholastic.

Phillips, Jayne Anne. Winter 2009. Interview by Paul Vidich. *Narrative Magazine*.

Pianta, Robert C., Karen M. La Paro, and Megan Stuhlman. 2004. "The Classroom Assessment Scoring System." *The Elementary School Journal* 104(5): 409–26.

Polacco, Patricia. 1994. *Pink and Say*. New York: Philomel Books.

Probst, Robert. 2004. *Response & Analysis*. Portsmouth, NH: Heinemann.

The Program in Narrative Medicine, 29 December 2010, College of Physicians and Surgeons, Columbia University www.narrativemedicine.org.

Quindlen, Anna. 2007. Foreword to *A Wrinkle in Time* by Madeleine L'Engle. New York: Square Fish.

Ray, Katie Wood. 2002. *What You Know by Heart: How to Develop Curriculum for Your Writing Workshop*. Portsmouth, NH: Heinemann.

Resnik, Lauren. 1995. "From Aptitude to Effort: A Foundation in Our Schools." *Daedalus, Journal of the American Academy of Arts and Sciences* 124(4).

Rosenblatt, Louise. 1938. *Literature as Exploration*. New York: Modern Language Association of America, 1995.

————. 1978. *The Reader, The Text, The Poem: The Transactional Theory of the Literary Work*. Carbondale, IL: Southern Illinois University Press.

Rylant, Cynthia. 1985. "Spaghetti." *Every Living Thing*. New York: Simon & Schuster Books for Young Readers.

Santman, Donna. 2005. *Shades of Meaning*. Portsmouth, NH: Heinemann.

Scavo, Susan Marie. 1999. "Food. Music. Memory." *What Have You Lost?*, ed. Naomi Shihab Nye. New York: Greenwillow Books.

Scholastic Guided Reading Programs. Scholastic, Inc. Accessed April 20, 2011 http://teacher.scholastic.com/products/guidedreading/fictions_z.htm.

Scholes, Roberts. 1985. *Textual Power: Literary Theory and the Teaching of English*. New Haven, CT: Yale University Press.

Seuss, Dr. 1957. *The Cat in the Hat*. Boston: Houghton Mifflin.

Sharmat, Marjorie Weinman. 2002. *Nate the Great*. New York: Delacorte Books for Young Readers.

Small, Mary. 1997. *A Pony Named Shawney*. New York: Mondo Publishing.

Smith, Doris Buchanan. 1973. *A Taste of Blackberries*. New York: HarperCollins Children's Books.

Sones, Sonya. 1999. *Stop Pretending: What Happened When My Big Sister Went Crazy*. HarperCollins Children's Books.

Spandel, Vicki. 2005. *The 9 Rights of Every Writer.* Portsmouth, NH: Heinemann.

Speare, Elizabeth George. 1983. *The Sign of the Beaver.* New York: Bantam Doubleday Dell Books for Young Readers.

Tatum, Alfred. 2009. *Reading for Their Life: (Re)Building the Textual Lineages of African American Adolescent Males.* Portsmouth, NH: Heinemann.

Willard, Nancy. 1993. *Telling Time: Angels, Ancestors, and Stories.* New York: Harcourt, Brace & Company.

Woodson, Jacqueline. 2000. *Miracle's Boys.* New York: G. P. Putnam's Sons.

Wyeth, Sharon Dennis. 1998. *Something Beautiful.* New York: Dragonfly Books.

Zolotow, Charlotte. 1972. *William's Doll.* New York: HarperCollins.

Books that English teachers can rely on

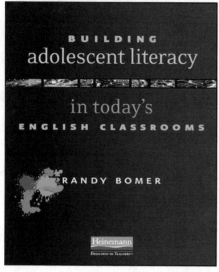

Grades 6–12 / 978-0-325-01394-7 / 2011 / 344pp / $36.00

Deciding what to teach in English class is more complicated—and more important—than ever. **Randy Bomer** provides an approach that works for today's adolescents, including how to:

- understand adolescents and their literacy needs through effective assessment

- give students opportunities to be motivated, critical, passionate readers and writers

- help adolescents be invested in literacy with a curriculum that connected them to the world.

Middle-school teacher **Donna Santman** shows how to teach the skills and strategies of comprehension and interpretation that allow students to stretch and empower their imaginations including guidance in:

- creating curriculum and lessons that teach habits of mind that support interpretation, like naming the ideas hiding in texts and thinking about perspectives from which to analyze those ideas

- teaching students to practice articulating their thoughts, exploring others' ideas, and interpreting texts

- assessing students' interpretive skills and moving them toward deeper and more meaningful interpretations.

shades of meaning

Comprehension and Interpretation in Middle School

DONNA SANTMAN
Foreword by RANDY BOMER

Grades 5–9 / 978-0-325-00664-2 / 2005 / 176pp / $22.00

DEDICATED TO TEACHERS™

CALL **800.225.5800** · FAX **877.231.6980** · VISIT **Heinemann.com**